The Practical Reiki Master – Book 2

Text Copyright © 2016 Mark A. Ashford Consulting Inc.
All Rights Reserved
Paperback ISBN Number: 978-1-988441-13-9
eBook - ISBN: 978-1-988441-75-7

1. Introduction

Reiki has a very ancient Shaman heritage.

The heritage dates to a time long before Buddhism became the official religion of Tibet in the 7th century AD, a very long time before the early 1800's and the discovery of the healing tradition in Sanskrit texts and Buddhist temples by Dr. Mikao Usui who is credited with bringing this wonderful heritage first to Japan, and then through his students, to Hawaii and the west.

The Shaman healing traditions assimilated by early Tibetan Buddhism, Yogic traditions, and the power of Sanskrit as a written language to pass the oral Shaman knowledge down through history to us today is documented here.

This book includes daily posts and observations appearing on our blog as well as tips and information on Reiki for both the attuned and those who are yet to be.

Mark A. Ashford
www.Markaashford.com
Information@markaashford.com

2. Table of Contents

1. Introduction 2
2. Table of Contents 3
3. List of Tables 5
4. New Moon 6
5. A New Moon and a Wish. 8
6. Are you Ready for a Cocoon? 9
7. Autumn 11
8. Connecting with Reiki 13
9. Challenging times and Reiki Principles 14
10. Gratitude is about saying thank you 16
11. Clearing Your Space 17
12. Reiki Healing Energy Bubbles 19
13. Happy New Year! 21
14. Happiness is all we want… 24
15. Growing Energy 25
16. Getting to know your guides and Angels 27
17. Personal Forgiveness and Gratitude 29
18. Five Principles of Reiki 31
19. Energetic Cleansing with a Full Moon. 31
20. Communication 34
21. Healing, Food, and Reiki 36
22. Intentions Slips 37
23. If We Allow It! 38
24. Setting Healthy Boundaries 40
25. Karma and Reiki 42
26. Let Go 44
27. Worries, Uncertainties, Worries and Uncertainty 45
28. Loving 47
29. Listen to your intuition, not your ego. 49
30. Mindset 50
31. New Year's Resolutions. 52
32. New Experiences and Reiki Energy 53
33. My Start with Reiki 54
34. Mother Earth of Gaia 56
35. More Energy is Coming 57

36.	Reiki Positivity Release stress	58
37.	Reiki and Home Life	60
38.	Reiki Healing	62
39.	Reiki Positivity Release stress	64
40.	Reiki for a Good Night's Sleep	66
41.	Reiki Personal Clearing	68
42.	Reiki Chakra Energy	69
43.	Reiki and Meditation	71
44.	Reiki Spring Cleaning	72
45.	Goals and Manifesting dreams	73
46.	Manifesting	75
47.	A Vision Board	76
48.	Reiki Vision Board	78

3. List of Tables

Table 1. Chakras, meaning and associated crystals 69

4. New Moon

The lunar cycle is every 29.5 days. Google the lunar cycle to see where you are in terms of the current cycle. Ideally, being close to the New Moon is best for this exercise. The New Moon, New things, New Hopes, New wishes. The full moon brings new wishes and hopes to fruition.

The moon is important. The moon is the light that made the night livable for the ancients, the nightly plunge into darkness was not so scary with the moon to shine down and illuminate the land. Over time, rituals and beliefs became associated with the Moon in its own right. Where it was in the sky, what phase of the moon all helped describe the progress of days, weeks, and a month. Astrology and the beginnings of astronomy soon took over as the human mind expanded and experimented with the way the world and the heavens worked.

The sun is too bright to look at unless you are looking at sunrise or sunset, but even then, you cannot look at it much after or before the final few minutes. This in part is why Druids and other ancient religions marked the Summer and Winter Solstices, at dawn, not Midday.

The new moon historically has been a time to look forward to new opportunities, new manifestation and new intentions. It has been a time to look backwards and discard what is not working, what has passed the part it is to play in your life.

You can think and dream about these things but to be most effective writing things down is best. Writing things down is a physical task, even if you type at the keyboard, you need to exercise your brain to get letters into the order required to write a word that can be read by anyone. The physical action of writing or typing engages your mind and thoughts. Those translate into letters and words. Words into sentences.

Now that you are actively thinking and acting – writing, you can bring energy and intention to the two things you need clarity on. What you are looking backwards on and what you are looking forward to.

I like the idea of having two pieces of paper, one with the heading "In with the New" and the other headed up "Out with the Old."

You may think that In with the New is most important, and it is, but Out with the Old is equally significant.

Think of a glass into which you put water to drink. If you drink half of the glass and want to drink more fresh water you can only top up the glass by as much as you have space for. If you tip away the old water, you have a complete glass that you can fill with fresh water.

Sounds simple, obvious. We do it every day. But our lives are the same, we can only have so much of anything at any one time. The Out with the Old is the list of things that will not make it into the next Moon phase.

Start with the piece of paper title Out with the Old.

Start making a list. One line to each thing that will not make it into the next phase. Number each one. If you have a lot, consider the list and see which are connected to people and places, and what is associated with things. Things are things you can sell, throw out, or pack away such as winter clothing.

People and places need a little study. Look at why and how a person or place will not be allowed into the next phase and carefully consider why. If you have been hurt in some way, why did you get hurt, did you allow it? How could you help yourself not get into the same situation again? Once you have figured that out, put what you have to do it at the top of the In with the New piece of paper or screen.

By putting what is required within you to change at the top of the new list, the more likely it is happen. Plus, the good coming in with the New cannot be as beneficial if you have not changed. But, if you were the cause of what needs to change, express your regret on that piece of paper, understand it and consider if you need to take any action. Add what you decide to the top of the In with the New paper, it is another part of the changes you need to make n yourself to allow the new moon and the coming phase to be happy and successful.

If you're Out with the Old includes people that have harmed you, release the energy the harm has inflicted on you. This is especially true if you have allowed the negative energy to grow and hurt you. Your ego mind enjoys nothing more than to feed off this energy and go over and over the same situation to magnify the hurt you have received. By releasing the cause, you prevent the ego mind from having anything to chew over and inflict itself on you, day after day.
By having these things at the top of the list, you can deal with them quickly and if you do it right, they should not be there at the next New Moon.

You are free to write down the new things you want to manifest in your life. Again, separating people and places from things will give you clarity as to how your life will change and what the impact on you will be.

At the end of the exercise for the New Moon, draw Cho Ku Rei over the two lists three times. If you have the ability to burn the Out with The Old paper, do so. Otherwise shred or tear it up. If it is a computer file, delete the file.

The last thing to do is clear your mind and relaxes as you look over the In with the New list.

5. A New Moon and a Wish.

New Moons are special events. They are very good for focusing our intention on manifesting new things in our lives. Whether it is something material, maybe a new car or deeply personal such as a relationship. A new Moon is a good time to concentrate on it and get your wish in tune with the phases of the moon.

It's very simple really. Yiu plant a wish in the rich energy of the Moon, Reiki energy and the wonderful energy of Mother Earth. These higher energies will look after the wishes on your list.

How to make a wish on a New Moon:

Take a piece of paper and draw the Power Symbol Chokurey, at the top in the center, at the top of each corner and at the bottom in the middle.

Make a list. Make it a simple list. This is your New Moon and a Wish. A new blue car, this is not the time for make and model information. Just the fact the car is new and it is blue.

On the reverse of the paper draw any symbols you are attuned too. If you are a Level One practitioner, you will not be attuned to any symbols. So, draw Chokurey. You are not attuned to this level of symbol; you are recording your contention for the symbol to add Reiki energy to your wishes.

With the finger of one hand, the one you write with. Draw Chokurey on the palm of each hand. Make sure your finger tip touches the palm so you can feel the symbol being drawn.

Place sheet of paper, unfolded between your hands. Close your eyes and visualize the symbols and penetrating the paper and your wishes.

If you have a garden, sprinkle some earth on the paper and seal the paper with the sprinkles in an envelope. As you do so, ask Mother Earth to help the wishes grow into what you have in mind for them.

6. Are you Ready for a Cocoon?

Life, contrary to what we believe about time is not a straight line, it is not linear. We count our birthdays, 20 follows 19 and 21 follows 20, but the way we grow and develop personally, how our internal spirit evolves changes sometimes by leaps and bounds. At other times, it develops slowly, almost methodically.

It is the time after a period of intense creativity, or action, when what we have been doing cannot continue as it has been, or even should continue, that we suddenly slow down and perceive what we call 'burn out.' Some call it "hitting a brick wall."

We stop and for some this is a crisis.

Without the sense of drive, without the sense of achieving, we feel lost, we sometimes do not understand why this has happened and we look for something we have done, or not done. Often, we feel we have failed.

I challenge the terms burn out, brick wall. I personally do not see this as a period of failure because we are not asking ourselves whether we believed the pace and intensity you were living at would last, could last, or should last? Did we think it was reasonable?

Life has a way of preventing you from continuing doing things that are not in your spiritual best interest. Trying and force it to continue is destructive to what you have achieved and delays what you could.

The "halt" may be leisurely, or it can be shocking.

A leisurely halt might expect, or even planned. For example, an actor in a production knows when their character will no longer part of the production, they know when that will be. But someone who has worked at a job, and they are let go, downsized, or fired that is a shock.

Being sensitive to the changes coming to our lives, and not focusing on the negative is difficult and stressing for many. But I suggest, I ask, that you focus on the positive when this happens. You are gifted an opportunity to develop and grow in a different direction. Accepting the change is important. Change is coming regardless of whether you organized it and anticipated it or not.

Imagine you are a bird, high in the sky, looking down on you and your life. What do you see? What is it about you that stands out the most? What defines you and what is it you are devoting your energy, yourself to?

Think of a caterpillar that spins a cocoon and enters it. It comes out as a butterfly. The caterpillar does not resist going in to the cocoon, it goes gladly. It may not know what it will turn in to, it just knows that the cocoon is the next step in its existence. You have achieved a lot as a caterpillar, but as a butterfly, you will be more beautiful, you will fly higher, and longer and further than the caterpillar could ever have done.

Be patient, do not wish for what has been to continue, instead, look at what is about to happen use your senses and ability to detect what the next phase will be. It is there, staring you in the face, you just have to stop wishing for the past to continue and be prepared to accept what in the future you will become.

7. Autumn

Reiki connects us with the universal energy, it connects us with all growing and living things which includes the seasons. The ancients knew about this and celebrated spring, when we plant crops and things, we want to grow through the summer so we can harvest them in the Autumn or Fall in North America. We celebrate the longest days of the year, in summer and in winter.

As the seasons change, so does our energy and connection with our inner self and that means our need for and connection to Reiki differs.

Autumn is the time of year when trees and all manner of growing things shed their leaves, go into hibernation, or die. It is a season that reminds us for the second time of the year to let go things that do not benefit us. Letting go things that do not benefit us is a seasonal thing. Like leaves and plants, relationships, friendships and connections must end and we should not be fearful of the change happening.

There will be new connections, new relationships, and new friendships, perhaps starting in the Autumn once the leaves have gone from the summer. These new relationships, and new friendships will grow and flourish, what grows in the depth of winter maybe deeper and richer than what blossomed during the summer now past.

Always look forward with optimism and be open. Ask your angels and guides for help to carry away your worries, worries that may prevent something new from coming into your life. Think of it in terms of the Autumn winds, they always seem to be stronger as they carry away the dead leaves. They can carry your worries too.

While we talk about leaves dying and falling from the trees, plants going into hibernation feel the trust in you that as the season appears to be less colorful and happy, the next year will bring back something equally colorful as what is passing. The Reiki energy is with you no matter what the situation, no matter what the season, it is just easier to see when everything is green, glowing and lush.

In the Autumn and winter make sure you connect to Reiki energy and understand that it is limitless and strong and touches every aspect of you. It makes you strong. Spend some time in a quiet space, perhaps a park bench, even a car seat with the window rolled down so that you can smell and hear and feel the energy of nature.

If you are attuned to Reiki, use the energy to clean your senses and your feeling. Believe in your own inner light, at the start of each day, place your hand over your heart and tell you how much you appreciate and love you. This is all about you. At the end of the day, do the same for all that happened that day. You are love yourself for how you handled that day. Perhaps start a self-Reiki session to ask the energy to fill and balance your chakras and take away your worries and concerns.

Reiki is natural energy that creates the life around us and in us. It will bring back the lush greenness next year, for now, it has gifts in the Autumn, and coming winter. They are more difficult to see. It is time to look.

The seasonal changes align you to Reiki energy if you will allow it, and reinforce your connection to it and yourself. Reiki learning and align you with your soul. It's not about how long you spend in nature; it's more about how aware you are when you do.

So, as the seasons change, as summer turns to Autumn and autumn to Winter, let go of things that no longer serve you. Recognize that seasons end is the opening for new winter wonders and a new spring next year. Reiki is there, all around you, and in you and you are part of the universal energy.

8. Connecting with Reiki

If you are attuned to Reiki you have a relationship to Reiki. That relationship is more than being a mechanic repairing cars. Reiki is an integral part of your being, of your personality and your soul.

You are a conduit for Reiki energy. In a sense you never really stop giving Reiki, even if you do not call it Reiki. You are living and breathing the essential source of life and love that is part of Reiki energy. In essence you are Reiki.

In this COVID-19 era, in person sessions can be difficult to conduct. Remote Reiki session where the Reiki Practitioner connects with another person without that physical in person relationship is key to helping others with Reiki energy. I always ask permission of the recipient to send them Reiki. It is not that Reiki is not intelligent and will help them if sent, but some people do not understand the feelings and results associated with receiving Reiki Energy.

Don't forget Reiki energy may help in the healing of the recipient or it may not. The outcome may be more or less than the recipient expects. It may also be unexpected and have a different focus than you intended but the ultimate goal is beneficial.

I once sent Reiki to someone who was under a lot of stress with work and a very sick mother in hospital. Elder brothers and sisters had "off loaded" their responsibility to the younger sister who bore this well but accepted Reiki to help her cope.

She woke up the next morning with a splitting headache and when asked what her duties to her mother would be that day, she loudly voiced her anger at bearing the responsibilities alone. The outcome by lunchtime was a considerable realignment of obligations and the head ache went away and never reappeared. Reiki energy had created a situation that sparked a rebalancing of the burdens, and admiration and love for the younger sister for all she had been doing without her siblings fully knowing.

Whether you use symbols or not in your Remote Reiki session is determined by how you are guided. It is also determined by your connection to Reiki. Some practitioners will use Reiki symbols, and other will not, some may only use symbols such as Cho Ku Rei the power symbol. If you are able to connect with reiki in a way that does not require symbols, then so be it – use that connection to the fullest. Explore the connection and develop it in a way that best suits you and how you practice. Be at one with reiki and it will tell you what is needed.

9. Challenging times and Reiki Principles

The COVID-19 virus has filled our minds and attention for weeks and months. We have been in lockdown as health workers tirelessly battle the infection. Social distancing keeps us from people and places we would like, no, love to go and be with. And, we may be opening up our towns cities and countries too quickly making a second and even third wave of infection inevitable.

Now we have riots in America. The images are real, of people, places and buildings and vehicles blazing. As connected as we are, these images repeat over and over. Repetition of the images breeds a callous disregard for the meaning behind them.

The undercurrent of all this is the economy and how we will make money to pay our bills, eat and live.

COVID-19 has and will continue to change many things about our world and lives, no least is the fact we will be living something that can infect and kill us until we get a vaccine. When we have the vaccine, there is worry at the back of our minds that when we do, COVID-20, and COVID-21 will appear.

In all of this, retaining our individual power is important. Protect it, and, retain it. Each of us as individuals are responsible for our essential energy, how we create it, how we use it, and how we keep it. Above all, do not take on the energies and thoughts of others who may be darker and less resilient than we are. Always, look to the light within us and feed it with care and attention.

A self-reiki session, especially if you are attuned to Reiki is important to help releasing the negative energy we are encountering in these times. If you are not attuned and cannot provide a self-Reiki session for yourself, book a remote session.

Dr. Usui established the Five Principles of Reiki:

… do not Anger. Do not let the situations we observe or encounter be things that make us angry. We have no control over them and we do not know or may not understand the importance someone places on something that can create offence in us. Do not make judgement and do not seek to take any action on what we see. Let it pass over and through us knowing that our energy, our power is within us and unchanged.

… do not Worry. Worry is part of our ego and our busy mind. It loves nothing more than to churn and exhaust our store of good energy by expending it on things we cannot change. If you catch yourself worrying about the line, whether the store will have all the supplies you need, let go of it!

… be Humble. Being Humble can mean not being proud or arrogant but rather being modest. Being modest can mean being free of vanity and self-importance. Being free of, or not being proud or arrogant. It does not mean you allow people to "walk over you" you have your own power and energy and can protect against such things from aggressive people, but you do not use that power to walk over others.

… be Honest with others. Do not represent yourself or your power as being something it is not. If you cannot help, say so, if you can, say so.

… Be Compassionate. Compassion is a feeling of sympathy for someone who has suffered misfortune or is in a state where we feel there is need to intercede and help lessen any burden or suffering, they are feeling. Compassion is not something we should allow to lessen our own energy and power. Draining our energy and power for the benefit of another has its limits and we need to recognize them and protect ourselves while doing what we can and is sensible for us, and the other person.

10. Gratitude is about saying thank you

Parents teach us to say thank you, or offer some other words of appreciation for something, it can be anything, that has helped us in some way.

I would say thank you to a friend at the gym who gives me the sports pages from their newspaper, I appreciate the pages because reading makes the time pass more quickly as I walk on the treadmill or peddle on the stationary bicycle.

It could be to the sales assistant who goes a little bit further searching for the item I want to buy and finds the last one in the store.

It could be my cat who wakes me up because she senses it is time for me to get up when I had forgotten to set the alarm the night before.

It can be someone who has stopped me doing something unwise, or dangerous, and has pointed me in a different direction saving me from injury.

Most often though, it is gratitude offered to my Guardian Angels. They have spoken to me, through my intuition and changed my course of action. Each evening when I leave work, I have several different ways I can drive home, but I ask that I be shown the quickest and safest way. It has never failed yet, but I always make sure I say "Thank you!"

That sales assistant who searched and found the last one in the store and saved me $100. A series of things directed me to the store that day, something I had not planned to do when I left work. It was something to add to my list of chores for the weekend.

I allowed the voice in my head take over, I turned at a traffic light and went to the store, I found an assistant waiting for me who was prepared to look for the last one in stock, and discover in the system, there were other considerable savings for me.

As I walked out of the store, I was happy and thankful to my Guardian Angels. I thanked them profusely. Then, they guided me to take a different way home. I expected it to be busy but it was surprisingly empty of traffic and most of the numerous traffic lights I passed through were green. I offered another thank you as I parked my car and headed in doors.

Guardian Angels and all our angels and Arch Angels are with us through every moment of our lives. They love us unconditionally and through our thoughts and intuition they help us immensely every moment of every day.

Although their love and help is unconditional, showing appreciation and gratitude helps us recognize the good things that happen, and good things can also be bad things not happening, which is just as important.
As you learn to thank your Guardian Angels for the good things they send as messages either directly or through our intuition, the more likely we are to recognize and act on other messages in the future and receive gifts and benefits as a result.

11. Clearing Your Space

Why would you clear your space? What is your space? What benefit is doing it?

Energetically, as we move through life, we collect emotional and spiritual baggage and toxins. These can be from people, places, and events.

We bring them home, but we can also bring them within ourselves. They affect our emotions, our thoughts, our intellect. They drag down the energy of our chakras and they can stir or ego.

Many years ago, before I engaged with my Angels and guides to fulfill part of my life purpose which was to become a Reiki Master and Teacher, I would occasionally find myself working with toxic people or in a toxic environment. As I sat in traffic driving home and odd moments when I was supposed to be relaxing watching TV I would mentally go over again and again events that had happened at work.

I would worry about what the next day would bring.

As a Reiki Master I am able to engage with my angels and guides to recognize these people and situations and negate the affect they have on me, even while they are happening.

I sit quietly, and ask Archangel Michael to sever any energy cords attached to my soul, spirit, aura, physical self or Chakras. I want him to cut the cords and destroy them. I then ask him to fill me up with pure white light and protect me with his energy.

I will do this at the beginning and end of the day, or after being somewhere or with someone I consider toxic. You can speak the short mantra or think it. Some people will "wipe their hands over their face, head and upper body as if they were brushing away cords or spider threads. I have said the mantra in a crowded elevator on my way to lunch after meeting with a particularly toxic individual.

I prefer to think of the cords I am cutting as if they were tentacles with suction cups that attach to things and hold on tightly. I see Michael removing the suction cups and cutting the tentacles which shrivel up and disappear.

You can bring these energy cords, even souls and spirits home with you. You may not see them, or, be aware of them, but they enter your home and stay with you. Freely absorbing your energy. In Tibet and other places where the belief in sprits and souls that have not moved on to their next life is more prevalent, houses will be regularly cleared and doors and windows energetically sealed to prevent these often dark and lower energies from entering.

If you have heard of smudging a house with White Sage, this is one of the traditional methods of banishing these entities.

Another approach is to engage with your angles and guides and ask them to help you banish these spirits and energies.

Ask Archangel Michael to protect you and anyone else in the home, especially animals. As you accomplish the clearing.

Hands in Gassho, I move from room to room, asking them to banish or evict souls and spirits that should not be present. I call out spaces where a spirit or soul may hide or avoid my actions. Such as, under the bed, behind the could, in the draws, behind the door. Anywhere a soul or sprit can hide, I call out for them to be gone!

I include connecting rooms, hallways, etc.

I also ask my angels and guides to seal windows and doors so that spirits and souls cannot re-enter the home. This is all exhaustive, take your time and be patient. Give yourself and your angels and guides time to do their work.

Traditionally, when smudging a space, you leave a window ajar, not necessarily wide open, but a way for the souls and spirits to leave. Do the same when you and your angels and guides are clearing your space.

12. Reiki Healing Energy Bubbles

Reiki Healing Energy Bubbles what are the and how can they help you, a Reiki Practitioner. As a practitioner, you are aware Reiki energy and the energy of the Archangels can come to you in different ways, and with diverse messages attached to it.

An energy bubble can be many things, each meaning different and valid for each practitioner. Generally, to me a Reiki energy Bubble something like a Reiki Energy Multi Vitamin with distinctive energies and strength of energy.

The bubble will take on a different color depending on who and why it is being created. There is a lot being prepared for the recipient so you have to clearly focus your mind and intention on the outcome you want.

To be open to this energy you need to be grounded, spiritually and emotionally. At this time of year, summer in Norther America, it is easy to find a park bench at my favorite spot by the lake and take off my sandals and let my feet connect me to grounding Reiki energy and Mother Earth, Gaia.

Be patient for the grounding energy to make itself felt. I usually find some tingling in my feet, especially my toes, and it moves up into my legs. The sense of being grounded is palpable.

Archangel Raphael is the healing Archangel. When preforming a Reiki session, remote or in person, asking for him to be present and to join in the session is always advantageous for the recipient. If the recipient if remote form you, therefore you are doing a remote Reiki session, draw the remote healing symbol Hon Sha Ze Sho Nen in the air in front of you as you focus your intention on the healing you are sending to the recipient.

This energy bubble you are creating either for yourself or another is an open bubble. There is no exclusion. If another Archangel appears, or a guide and they want to participate, all the better their energy adds to the potency of the energy you are creating.

The intention of healing is to heal, so visualize the person healed and removed from the discomfort and any pain they are in. If you visualize an outcome, such as manifestation of wealth or abundance, in your mind see it completed.

If manifestation means something for yourself, not only be clear in your intent to manifest but also tell the universe you are open to receive exactly what you ask for or something better. Declining something is to send the universe a message is dislike and rejection. Always be open to receive what the universe sends you, not what you dream you would like.

As you close the session, seal it with Cho Kho Rei, the Reiki Power Symbol to give the bubble and all that is in its potency and energy. Give the bubble your intent that the bubble be delivered to the recipient, or yourself if it is for you.

I usually visualize the bubble being an energy source for the Root Chakra. Bind it to the root Chakra so that all the energy in the bubble washes over and permeates the Root Chakra. The energy flows upward form the root to all the chakras and channels in the body.

If there are any energy stream from one Chakra to the next, Archangel Metatron and Archangel Raphael together can be called on to remove the blockages.

If one Chakra in particular needs healing energy, you can send the bubble of healing energy to that chakra directly. The bubble will contain what the chakra needs to heal.

Raphael is associated with green and the emerald crystal, not the gemstone, is his crystal. Raphael is associated with the Heart chakra. You can use the crystal by placing it over the Heart Chakra, or if remote, visualizing the crystal there and glowing.

13. Happy New Year!

Happy New Year! Yes, that is correct, New Year's brings the opportunity to clear away the past month, the past year, the past few years, the past decade.

What we are talking about here can be at any time of the year.

If you keep a daily journal, close it, mentally and spiritually, and mark it as sealed. You are not going to be looking in it anymore not sneaking back to see what you thought of such and such a person or how you felt after someone new came into your life or they left it. After sealing it you are going to make sure it is gone for good by shredding it, tearing it up, or brining it if you have that option.

Spiritually sealing it helps you forget. What is gone is done and cannot be changed.

Start a new journal, a clean sheet, a clean book, a clean page on the word processor.

Now is the time to dream. Dream whatever you want and to record your dreams.

Sit quietly, with a cup of tea, coffee, a cold drink or some other favorite drink. This is a time to slow down and connect with your guides and angels. It is a time to come to terms with what it you desire, wish for, would like to manifest.

The lunar cycle is every 29.5 days. Google the lunar cycle to see where you are in terms of the current cycle. Ideally, being close to the New Moon is best for this exercise. The New Moon, New things, New Hopes, New wishes. The full moon brings new wishes and hopes to fruition.

Think of the abundance you wish to receive, in:

Prosperity/Finances
Health/Vitality
Family Relationships
Relationships and Love
Career Opportunities
Shelter/home
Protection
Peace
Support

This list is not exhaustive, feel free to add what is missing but is important to you. But remember., this is for you, it is personal to you.

After you have made your list, think carefully about what you have circled. If you wish to manifest a new car, think of the things that are important to you and do research to be clear on what it looks like; make, model, color, number of doors, cargo capacity, towing capacity, engine size, interior colors. This is your dream, your desire, your wish, your hope it is what you want to manifest.

If it is a person, how tall are they, what color eyes, hair, age, background and any other attribute of your ideal person that you can think of, is important to you and you want to manifest in them.

If this sounds like a vision board, you are correct. It can be a vision board together with pictures and even sounds, if it is on a computer or smartphone.

If you are attuned to Reiki, add Reiki symbols to the page, make them into an attractive and powerful border. Say the Power symbol name out loud. As you do this, and when you are finished, hold the book, paper, images you have collected in your hands or lay your hands on them, close your eyes and say the power symbol again.

It is important that what you write, the images you collect and the wishes you want to manifest are wholly and entirely yours. Not anyone else's, YOURs and yours alone.

Balance in all things, including what you want to manifest. We are taught it is better to give than to receive and many of us carry a burden of not feeling worthy of the great things we can wish for here. Understand that Balance is required in all things. If you have any doubts about your worthiness to receive what you are asking to be manifest. Stop yourself. Fugitively and emotionally, "spit those thoughts out."

You are worthy, having a nice home, car, holiday home, lover, a healthy body, success, you are worthy of all these things. Do not hold back or resist making the declaration of your needs and only your needs.

When you go to sleep that night, before you drop into a deep peaceful sleep, imagine what it would be like in the home, the car or being with the person you have asked to be manifested. Put your heart into the thoughts and wishes now. Any negative thoughts that are blocking you form thinking positively about what you manifest, banish them.

Thoughts of who cares, why bother, what difference will it make, or if it has not arrived by now, it never will. These are negative thoughts and if they are your thoughts, banish them. If they are not yours, they have come from people you know, then be prepared in the future not to accept these comments. Be prepared to rebut them and put the speaker in their place.

Ask your angels and guides to help you remove these negative thoughts by taking them away.

If you are attuned to the Tibetan Master symbol, use it to emotionally cleanse yourself of these habits. Print out or draw a large Tibetan Master symbol on a piece of paper and place it in a large Freezer bag that s sealed and place it under your pillow and "sleep on it."

Each night, take it out and trace it with your finger, say the name three times, and state your intention to remove the negative thoughts and habits. Put it back under your pillow and fall asleep.

In the morning, give yourself time to once again think of what it is you want to manifest and say the Power Symbol over your thoughts and desires.

Lastly, two things.

Your desire to manifest things may not happen within one moon cycle, allow the universe time to bring you what you are asking for.

The other is to not be disappointed if what manifests is not exactly like what you pictured. A car can be a different color and a house may be in the middle of the street, not at the end. It may be two floors, rather than one.

You have received what you need, not necessarily what you want.

14. Happiness is all we want…

Happiness, we all want some happiness in our lives. It does not matter what creates it, it could be baking, planting flowers or vegetables, or completing a long bicycle ride. Whatever it is, something makes us feel good about ourselves, what we are doing or simply, just being alive.

When we are happy, that is the time to show gratitude to life, but especially what made us feel happy in the first place. Being and showing gratitude changes your life. What you are thankful for becomes clearer in your mind.

When we are happy and we want to show gratitude. You can simply say, something like, I am pleased, I am happy, I enjoy that… Another way to do is to write down what it you are happy about. The act of writing, holding a pen and shaping the letters on a piece of paper, reinforces what it is you are happy about and what has brought you to that enjoyable state. Of course, you can type at a keyboard.

The point is to have a physical record of happiness and gratitude.

Put the pieces of paper into a box, a draw, or a glass jar if you have used small pieces of paper.

If you are attuned to Reiki, can draw the symbols, over the container in which you have stored your notes. If you are not attuned, think of the best sunrise you have experienced. It doesn't matter when the sunrise occurred, just that you witnessed it. In case you have not seen a sunrise, you can think of now, think of music.

Feel free to add to the notes in the container. Moments of a happy occasion, a holiday, a party, a celebration of some kind such as a wedding, a birthday. Or, an award. These things and the memories add energy to the energy in your notes.

Gratitude creates more happiness and things to be grateful for. Abundance starts to manifest, the type of abundance that creates more gratitude.

From time to time, especially if you are feeling unhappy, open the container and read through the notes, take out the mementoes, look at the pictures if there are any. Hold them and let Reiki together with the look and feel of the keep sakes bring happy memories and gratitude back into your life and sweep away the unhappiness you are feeling.

15. Growing Energy

ature is a wonderful, interconnected and incredibly diverse system of growing things - Growing Energy - I call it! Did you know that with every plant or things that grows there is a nature angel encouraging it to grow and give it strength and energy?

Being out in nature, amongst the tree's grasses, plants and flowers is a way to connect just with nature in the bigger sense but all the small things that make up what you see, feel and smell. Having something growing in your house is was to connect with growing things. Let's be clear on that statement. We are not talking about cut flowers, although they are beautiful and we care for them while their blooms are bright and full, they are already dead. The roots and soil around the roots are no longer with them.

To have something growing in your home means to have soil, a plant and to be watering it and giving it the sunlight and other nutrients, it needs to meet the expectation of the nature angel hovering over it.

That growing plan will bring positivity with it. It will be good for you and what you do to take care of it will also be something else good for you. If you are sensitive to Reiki and spiritual energy, they will not bring positivity to you but they will also bring energy. If you are attuned to Reiki, this will be a bi-directional transfer of energy – from you to them and from them to you. If you have a garden, that will be all the more so. If a plant struggles to grow, it will show you. And, like a human recipient, you can send Reiki energy to it.

Send the reiki energy to them once or twice a week or if the plant seems to be struggling, every few days until it starts to improve.

The energy that plants provide to a space or to you are enhanced by the physical fact that plants are source oxygen – which we all need.

Various folk cultures and traditions assign symbolic meanings to plants. Although these are no longer commonly understood by populations that are increasingly divorced from their old rural traditions, some survive. In addition, these meanings are alluded to in older pictures, songs and writings. New symbols have also arisen: one of the most known in the United Kingdom is the red poppy as a symbol of remembrance of the fallen in war.[1]

For an extensive list of plants and their associated meanings visit Wikipedia at -
https://en.wikipedia.org/wiki/Plant_symbolism

The list does not include all plants obviously! My mother loved and cared for Afrikan Violets which are native to Tanzania, she could encourage the flowers to bloom year-round. If you are interested in brining plants into your environment, indoors or out, do some research first to understand what the plant needs. Afrikan Violets for example, like a lot of light but not direct sunlight. Soil should be a good quality potting mix, and kept moist and humidity should be high if possible, with temperature never below 15.5c or 60f.

---

[1] Wikipedia, "Plant Symbolism."

One other side effect if you have a garden is the improvement in your garden and your ability to help plants grow and thrive.

Bibliography

Wikipedia. "Plant Symbolism."

16. Getting to know your guides and Angels

Messages from your guides and angels come in the form of Intuition.

Listen to your intuition, not your ego.

The ego is:

An integral part of our soul. It comes with the soul when we are born and it will leave when we pass on.

It is that part of us that helps protect and guide us through the material world.

It protects us by giving us a sense of what we should not do, or what we should do given a particular situation. For example, I would never climb 60 feet up a tree, but as a scuba diver, looking over the some of the dive boat at 60 feet of depth. I did, and still do, find that exciting.

The ego test us apart from other people, the clothes we wear, the computer we use, where and how we live, the car we drive, where and what we do when we go on holiday… the list goes on and on.

The soul is power, packed with creative, life and expresses itself in energy and dedication. My time diving, took me into many realms; the physics and physiology of diving, history, medical knowledge, education and study, time and money. All of this happened within two years of a relationship ending that blocked these expansive bursts of growth and energy.

The ego can be slow to change. If it is slow to change it is because of its need for evidence and proof before that a change will be good for us. This can lead us to over think things as well as not take a risk to change. In hindsight if we accepted the risk we see that it was probably not as great a risk as the ego made it appear.

Some of the things that led me into diving and eventually being an instructor and opening a dive business were:

- Self Esteem – I liked and enjoyed diving, but as an instructor I had a role to play and people looked up to me
- Self-worth – because people looked up to me, I felt I had more value
- Self – The process of becoming an instructor and the feeling of increased self-worth increased confidence in myself and my capability

All of these things meant I was apart from the crowd of people who did no scuba dive and more importantly, were not instructors.
I was happy that I was doing something special and was no longer part of the crowd. And yet, if people were not involved in diving no one looking at me would know I was involved or that I had an elevated role.

If I had held back and not moved on to complete the courses and training that made me an instructor, I would not have been happy. Holding back my gifts, my talents, or the truth about myself, would not have made me happy, on the contrary, I would have been unhappy and unhappiness creates pan in our soul and our existence. It makes someone who has the potential to be a leader into someone who is a follower, that person is then submissive and just following everyone else.

STOP IT!!!! Listen to your heart, listen to your energy body, to your soul.

The ego has a role to play in our lives, it needs to be retrained but we need to have control over it, not be under its control.

Learn to act on your intuition and bring it to the front of your attention.

Intuition is the name we give to ideas and things that appear to us, and we talk about accepting them or seizing the opportunity our intuition tells us is there.

Intuition is our angels and guides speaking to us. A part of our self-healing is for each day to be a day when we learn about our own, personal, angels and guides, the roles they play in our lives and what they can do for us, the more intuitive ideas and opportunities appear and the closer we get to our soul and our purpose in this existence.

17. Personal Forgiveness and Gratitude

ersonal Forgiveness and Gratitude are part of the way you heal from past spiritual or emotional injuries. We all encounter spirit and emotional injuries. They can be personal or career related.

A personal relationship injury could be a divorce. After being with a partner for years, perhaps having children, and then discovering the connection is no longer there, that who was your partner now no longer sees you as being their companion can be heart wrenching. Or, working for a company for years, giving time, and emotional energy to make everything you are doing successful but then hearing you are no longer needed, your job has been ended and you are to leave, can be damaging to your emotional well-being.

When these things happen in life, taking responsibility for your life can be difficult. It is easier to give my life and energy away to others in the form of complaints and blame.

The first best thing to do is to give your anger and concerns to your angles and guides. Anger is a consuming energy that draws from your spiritual well but does not return anything. Concern is the same, it is just another word to describe a busy worrying mind that likes to churn and anguish over things that cannot be changed. You need to be rid of these draining energies and look to new things, new hopes, new desires, new opportunities.

As you look forward to new experiences and new successes, and new relationships, you also need to spend some time forgiving the situations that are now not part of your life. The personal break up, forgive yourself for any part you played in it. Forgive your partner for what happened then. The close that chapter in your book of life. Turn the page. Move the book mark to a new section, and continue from there.

If it was the loss fo a job, there is a reason for it. Situations change, the impact of competition on a company changes it needs and the way things are done and in the end the company must try and survive the changes. This doesn't change the hurt and pain for "no longer being needed" but you need to see the value you gave and how you were successful, when you were successful and be happy about that. The close that chapter in your book of life. Turn the page. Move the book mark to a new section, and continue from there.

Be open to new opportunities and changes, walk with your head up and not looking down. Be grateful to your angels and guides for taking the burden of your worries and sorrows from your mind and your shoulders.

Reiki is very supportive in situations when life takes a bad turn. If you are attuned to Reiki, settle down and let Reiki energy pass through you and refresh your chakras. Refresh your mind and your energy. In your quite space, draw Chu Ku Rei, the power symbol, and Sei He Ki. Sei He Ki is used for mental healing, accessing the subconscious and calming the mind. The translations mean "as above, so below" and represents Divine Source and human coming together. The use of this symbol is to address the emotional component behind physical diseases or energy blocks. This symbol is intended to calm the conscious mind and allow the subconscious memories of pain or trauma to come to the surface and be released.

Another adaptation is the Sei He Ki Chiryo Ho technique. It is a powerful way to release and transform unwanted habits, attitudes, and addictions. By the way, worry about things you cannot change is an addiction! The "worry or depression" habit may reside on more than one level of a person's Being. Sei He Ki Chiryo Ho works by planting a suggestion or activating a thought into the subconscious mind, enabling the mind to re-program and experience the vibration of this new thought pattern.

As you learn to heal and move on, be grateful for the changes taking place within you. Express your gratitude in your mind and say it to yourself every morning and evening. The changes are within you and you want to place your hand over your heart and tell yourself, you love yourself for all that has happened since you were sad and confused and hurt. You are glad you put those things behind you.

Life is a journey, a journey where each step has something to learn. Take the lesson, the instructions and the learning for what it is, not what your over active worry mind creates.

If you are not attuned to Reiki, book a session with a Reiki practitioner. Before the session starts, discuss what has brought you there and how you feel. Do not concern yourself with the outcome, Reiki can take care of that. Let Reiki help you, lead you and change you for the better, not just with how you are now, but set you on the path to being where you need to be in the future.

18. Five Principles of Reiki

These simple principles were created by Dr Usui after he had started practicing in the Beggar quarter of Tokyo.

The five Principles of Reiki are:

Also included in the principles of Reiki is the notion of Gratitude - "Just for today, I will be grateful."

Gratitude is a powerful thing. When we receive anything, showing gratitude to the giver is as good for ourselves as it for the person to know we are grateful for what they gave to us. It helps us to feel special and appreciated and that increases our spiritual vibration.

One thing I do every morning is to create a new page with the date in my Journal. This is a record of dreams; aspirations and hopes for what I am doing and things I am grateful for. It starts the new day and also ends the previous day. It is also a great way to start the day, like a clean slate.

Here are some ideas to express gratitude for, and a way to do it that is easy to remember.

Write down "I am grateful for the blessings of the universe. I am grateful for the gifts of… [then fill in the blank with what you are grateful for].

Waking up in the morning – I think we are all grateful for a new day in our lives.

Our Bodies. Now you may be unhappy with how you look, how you feel, but your physical body is the container in which your soul experiences each day. To be blunt, without your body, you would be dead so be grateful!

Air, sunshine and chirping birds and animals around us including our pets.

That we have someone to love. We all have someone to love, we love ourselves, we love us, we treasure us.

Food and water, are forms of abundance. Be grateful for them and be grateful for other forms of abundance such as material wealth and things that make our lives more comfortable.

Jobs, work, pleasure, friends, parents, all are things or people we can be grateful for.

Above all, the presence of Reiki in our lives. It is enriching intellectually and spiritually, and if we practice, it is a gift we give to others. So, be grateful for Reiki and the fact you can give, share, help others with Reiki energy.

19. Energetic Cleansing with a Full Moon.

Each morning I start the day with a shower. I love the water running over me, I especially love the temperature of the water at different times of the year, cool in the hot sunny weather, and warmer when it is cold and wintry.

After breakfast and before I dress to go out, I sit quietly and meditate mindfully for a few minutes. I slow and close off my busy mind that is planning inextricably for the day ahead, stirring emotions and thoughts about things that may never happen. Planning for all kinds of eventualities that also may never happen.

I never doubt that during the day I will silently accumulate unwanted, and perhaps dark energies from people and places I spend time in. If I allow them, those unwanted and dark energies will affect my lifestyle.

So, I ask Archangel Michael to be present and to use his sword to cut any energy cords attached to me and to fill me with his bright white light and surround me with his protective shield.

Then, I am ready to get dressed and get out into the world.

When I come home. I shower again, it is symbolic of washing away the dirt and grime of the day. Yes, office work can be grimy. Grime can be emotional if you are in a place that is unhappy.

Just as I never doubted, I would collect unwanted and dark energies from people and places I encounter during the day. I now sit quietly, meditating mindfully. Casting off those energies but also clearing out my mind. The evening is my own, I am not prepared to allow my busy ego mind to side track the enjoyment of the time with people I care about and doing what I enjoy doing.

I ask Archangel Michael to be present and to use his sword to cut any energy cords attached to me and to fill me with his bright white light and surround me with his protective shield. I am determined nothing will be attached to me and sap the emotional energy of my soul.

iCal on my computer is linked to a calendar of phases of the moon. My computer also runs an app with more detailed information about the moon, its phases, and position of the planets and the astrological signs.

As the planets, the Earth and the Moon move around the sky, they influence our souls and energy levels. If you are attuned to Reiki, the sense of energetic change they bring will be surprising at first but familiar as many more full moon cycles repeat.

The combination of daily spiritual clearing and cleansing in the morning an evening is magnified at the full moon. Not only is the cleansing amplified, shifting our consciousness in order to elevate our frequency bodes well for us if we focus on manifesting a better future for ourselves. This is a conscious decision to use the abundant full moon energy to bring peace, love, and joy to our lives and attain our goals and manifest my dreams.

Use your Reiki sensitivity to channel the full moon energies with awareness and mindfulness.

Each night, before I go to sleep, I ask my Archangels to clean and align my Chakras. But at the full moon, when Archangel Michael has cut and destroyed the energy cords that have attached themselves top me during the day, I ask for him to remain, stand guard, and cleanse the space I am in while I work with Reiki energy amplified by the full moon.

If I can be outside and the weather is suitable, I stand with bare feet on the grass. In this way I can connect with Mother Earth which grounds me, the connection stabilizes me as I connect more powerfully with limitless Reiki energy.

In the summer months it is sunny until a lot later and the brightness is greater than the reflected light of the moon. Visualize the full moon, as you ask for your guides and angels to be present as you think about the cleansing rays of light passing over and through your Chakras, your Aura, and through the Reiki energy you are channeling.

This cleansing adds to what you completed earlier.

Take a moment to once more mindfully meditate on the energy and cleansing that is and has taken place. At this moment is not just about your breathing that is helping you to meditate, it is all the cells, and tissues in your body.

At the end of the session, thank your guides and angels for being present. Walk around, you are still grounded but not rooted to any one spot.

Finally, Thank Archangel Michael for standing guard over the session and get ready to settle down and take it easy, if you can prepare and go directly to bed, that is even better. Do so, knowing you have severed all energy cords and used the power of a Full Moon for a deeper and more powerful energetic clearing.

20. Communication

They say we are what we eat… If that is the case, then what and how we communicate is also who we are. In today's world that is a complex subject. We communicate using, smart phones, computers, TV and radio. Often just naming a medium such as a smartphone does not cover what comes to us through it. There is person to person messages through SMS and messaging apps, as well as news media apps and apps that provide a digest of what is in many different news media.

All of what we do and say through these tools and media is energy, either we are absorbing from it, or giving to it. Depending on our role at work we may be a giver or taker through our devices. It is also true that working through electronic devices, like them, we are always "on." Out email inbox is always set to receive, and our chat window is always open to a quick connection.

To help with all the communication channels, staying organized and deleting files, folders, and pictures etc. that are of no use to us. For example, I sued to collect images for a vision board, but I never created the vision board, so the images were never used. Are they still relevant, is the vision board still required? If the vision board is not needed, at least in the form I once thought of it, delete the "idea" and start again and delete the images.

It is easy to collect things our laptops and not organize them, at work we are usually organize our files and information so that we can find thigs easily. Do that at home and on your personal devices.

When we have to hunt for things we need, we use up a lot of energy.

Email and chat messages are one of the worst offenders. When my mother passed away, I went through the draw in the sideboard where she stored letters she wanted to save to look back on, "if I need to." She lived in the generation where you wrote a letter, folded, it, put it in an envelope, put a stamp on it and mailed it in the way to work or when out shopping. Because of that effort and the time, it took for the mail to deliver the letter, writing to someone took time and required a lot of thought.

The simple act of buying the supplies to create a letter and the stamp made you think about what it was you wanted to say, why, and how. Email and SMS messages no longer carry that level of commitment. You can simply type, and send. The number of times we send messages that have little importance can be incredible. Learn how to differentiate these, and delete them.

BTW, when I say delete them, I mean delete them from the trash bin on your device as well, until you do that, the communication is never really gone and it still has a hold over you.

Take a moment to look through your contacts, are there any you have not communicated with for while? A long while, maybe years? Delete them.

While we are on the subject of looking through our contacts, include social media, people we have "friended" but who were never real friends in the sense you shared something with them. After years of membership in clubs and societies, I find I have collected the contact details of people who may no longer be members but who I have no connection without side the club. So, why are they still there?

One thing I recommend, when you receive a telemarketing call on your smartphone, and it is annoying, block the caller so they cannot annoy you again in the future. Not to block them is to allow them to come back and consume another small measure of your energy and to worry.

Update any profile pictures you are using. Old pictures, attract old energy and they radiate "old" use an up to date images that says more about who you are now.

As we are so dependent on our devices, devices that contain batteries to store energy so they do a service for us, make sure they are fully charged so that they are ready to do what we want. I use a separate rechargeable keyboard and mouse for all my typing. I charge them overnight when I do not need them, that is they are being readied for a new day while I am asleep.

We have been talking about tools, inanimate objects. Every morning before I do anything, I talk to my guides and ask them to "monitor, my thoughts, speech, behavior, and writing and edit as appropriate." The intention here is that all of these actions have someone look over them and help me communicate effectively and simply.

Sometimes, it is not just about what we say, but whether we need to say it at all! I used to compose emails and other messages without the address of the person it was intended for on the To: line. The messages were sometimes blunt and expressed what I felt rather than what I should say. If I pressed send by accident, the message would not actually be sent. Since I have my guides looking over my shoulder, I find I do not do that anymore, I have no need to.

At the end of the day and before going to bed, I thank my guides for "monitoring, my thoughts, speeches, behavior, and writing and editing as appropriate." Gratitude is always important. Your guides can help you use your laptop, smartphone and any other devices effectively and for the best use of your energy and to help you in managing the energy you receive from others through them.

Just as my mother had a draw of letters, she felt she might need to refer back to, those letters became out of date, old, and yellowed with time. Electronic files may not get yellowed, but they are old, and no longer relevant. Either delete or archive them away, the energy they are absorbing by you seeing them is doing you no good.

21. Healing, Food, and Reiki

Food, good nutritious food, not the junk, sugary foods we often eat is the fuel our bodies need in order to make us energized and successful. It is hard to do all the things we do on a good day if we feed ourselves junk which provides energy only for a short time.

One of the things we can do is to put some of the essential goodness of the universe into our food before we eat it. Draw Chu Ku Rei, the power symbol over the plate before you start, and, if you did not prepare the food, as you start to draw the symbol, think to yourself, "I am clearing this plate of food of any energies it may have acquired before it reached me."

At the last stage of drawing Chu Ku Rei, in your thoughts, add the intention that the food will boost the healing of anything in you that needs healing, and that it will also give you the energy to complete the day energetically and how you want to. As you complete drawing the Reiki Power symbol, make the last words emphatic and powerful.

This as one profound benefit. If you are like me, then there are times, especially when I am at work that I literally inhale my food because there are other things I want to need to do at lunchtime. Drawing Chu Ku Rei, clearing the food and imbuing energy and emphasis in to it slows you down and makes you enjoy the meal that much more. A meal is to be enjoyed; it is not a challenge.

As you complete your meal consider the intention you gave to the food. Be patient with the results. As with all intentions and healing cycles, the intention may not manifest right away, and it may not be in the form you imagine or ask for. Be patient and be accepting of the outcome the universe gifts you.

As you end your meal, thank your angels and guides and the universe for the opportunity to eat the meal and look forward to the energy and strength the food infused with universal, intelligent energy has provided.

22. Intentions Slips

The definition of "Intention" is:

- the end or object intended; purpose.

Intention Slips - when we talk about our intentions for the future, they can be anything. Big or small, complex or simple, they are things we want to happen in the future. Many of us think of our intentions using words like manifest or manifestation.

We create vision boards, we cut out pictures and paste them on the boards and we write lengthy descriptions to ourselves. We read them over and over again. We put them in plastic bags and keep them under our pillows so we can "sleep on them."

Intuition slips are simpler. Slips of paper on which we write our intention or what we want to manifest. The descriptions are far simpler. A simple sentence without punctuation.

If we are attuned with Reiki, we draw symbols on the back of the slip of paper. Then, we put the slips in our Intentions box, some call it a God box. The box can be as simple as a shoe box, or something an Amazon shipment came in.

Periodically, open the box and take the slips out every come of weeks. Look the lips over, and if any of them have been realized, leave them out. Our others that have not realized, back.

More important or larger things like a new house, getting married, you have to find the right person first! Having a baby, those take a little longer, three to four months, even six months is a good gauge for when to check the box and review what is in it.

You may even have two intention boxes, one fo things that will take longer, and one for those that can manifest more quickly.

Be patient with the intention boxes. Just because something can take longer, three to four months doesn't mean that I can't happen a few days after you put the slip in the box.

One format for the intention you write is to declare you have an intention, what that intention is, and thank Reiki for the energy to make the intention manifest. Remember, you are engaging Reiki Energy to help bring this intuition into reality. It is not blind hope. As you wrote the Reiki symbols on the back of the slip, also write them on the box lid so they are what you see when you pick up the box. Write the symbols on the underside of the lid so that Reiki Energy is looking down on the slips.

23. If We Allow It!

If we allow it anger and disappointment to stay in our lives, it will slowly eat away at us. Become what we think and feel, rather than the other way around. When I was attuned as a Reiki Practitioner, something new came into my life. An energy that helped me shed the worries and concerns, it allowed me to become peaceful and accepting and appreciative of what life gave to me rather blaming and unhappy if what I received was less than what I felt I was worth or due.

Over the years there had been many things that had been wonderful and engaging but also things that seemed like disappointments. The latter were like coats of paint, applied over, and over again, in different colors to some beautifully carved wood. As the layers of paint build up and up, the sharpness and wonder of the carving becomes blunted and less clear. The carving in losing the clarity of shape and design becomes less attractive to look at.

Reiki energy on clearing away the layers of disappointment restored the beauty of the carving to the light of day. Once again, its beauty was on show, once again, the carving could breathe.

The worries that upset my stomach were gone, the muffled throat chakra was speaking clearly and could be heard, the Heart Chakra beat more slowly.

There are of course two ways to experience Reiki, the simplest way is to book a Reiki session and receive it in either an in person or remote session. The other it to become attuned to Reiki and experience Reiki through the attunement process, Ultimately, when you are attuned to the highest level you will be able to perform self-Reiki.

With a new perspective, I could see why I was angry and why angry people and situations came into my life. I could see why the natural progression of life angered me.

Through self-Reiki old events, people and places that had created anger, frustration and seemed to magnify the disappointments I felt I were coming to me were still there, as clear as they had been all along, but now there was no pain associated with them. As my experience with self-Reiki grew stronger and more proficient, the less and less those old memories meant to me. And, if I encountered a person from those memories again, they did not create a sense of anger. I had been immunized from their anger, they were simply just a person that I had once known and lost connection with.

As I started to look back on my life, and compared it to what was happening now, I realized less and less angry people and places were being brought into my life. Being angry tends to create angry words and expression, angry behavior creates situations that can only create angry outcomes, situations and people. This made me very happy. The cycle of anger and angry people and toxic situations had ended.

This is not magic! It is Reiki. Will it stop you coming into contact with toxic people, especially at work, no. But it will help with your response, and it certainly will help with how these people and situations don't affect me. Like lightening, they strike my lightening rod which is Reiki and dissipate straight into the ground. At the end of the day, in my self-Reiki session, I look back and completely wash the situation and person away. If they come back the next day, I can deal with them again, in the same way while knowing how I must change things to rid myself of them and the situation.

Reiki is about the universal energy that is available to all of us, our soul chose to reincarnate in order to learn and experience. Our life path is the path we are walking for the soul to do experience. Reiki and that universal energy helps the life path to be less rocky and for the charisma of our soul to be less muted, less like the carving that has lost its shape and definition. The journey is about experience and learning, not how much baggage we can carry that has no value.

24. Setting Healthy Boundaries

Setting Healthy Boundaries with people is one of the best things you can do for yourself with the help of Reiki.

Some people refer to boundaries as a form of self-protection, a way of building a wall that keeps certain people, places, and events out of their personal space. This is an example of their self-respect; this reassurance of self-esteem helps remove negativity from life. The end result is they are happier in the knowledge their space will not or cannot be impinged on.

If you are attuned to Reiki, using the universal energy in Reiki to help set these boundaries is powerful and mysterious.

Think for a moment how you feel when someone imposes their will on you. They have it in their mind that events in your life should proceed at a pace they set and have no regard for your feelings, emotions or expectations. You are not at someone else's beck and call; you are not a skivvy to their beck and call. I know from experience that I do not like and resent people who have this opinion of me. I resent the manipulation they try to impose when they feel their control slipping.

It is important to remember that people learn from you how it is they are to treat you. It is you and you alone who are in charge of your life. When you make that known, you have established your boundaries, boundaries that keep you ascending your own vibrational ladder.

Reiki is a powerful tool for helping to set and maintain boundaries. Reiki works for the greatest good of all, and ego cannot influence Reiki. As a Reiki Practitioner, we are a conduit for the flow of Reiki Energy. We do not decide what it does or where it goes, it is intelligent so let Reiki energy do its thing, let it improve our lives.

Boundaries can be created using Reiki in many different ways.

Learn to say No! No, is not selfish. It tells others that what they are asking or indirectly hinting at it suggesting does not work for you, is not something you want to do or be a part of. No does not require an explanation. Stand firm on No if you really mean it and would be unhappy if you said yes!

If you know you will have to say no in a meeting or Infront of a group of people, find a moment when you can practice the scene, who says what and how and why. Do this with closed eyes and with a clear call to your Reiki guides for strength and clarity about what you are going to do in the meeting.

Also, think about the Throat Chakra. You will be speaking this Chakra is important. It needs to be clear, balanced and full of energy.
In today's world, it is often the case that we will have to speak for ourselves without the other person being present. It could be a phone call, or telephone conference call. It could be an email, or a video conference call. Again, preparation is similar to the steps described previously only this time it is not a one-to-one meeting but a group. Make your statement clear and politely, do not engage in any verbal or other challenges. Tell them what your boundaries are, what you accept and what you will not. If you are speaking give Reiki Strength to your Throat Chakra. Even if you

are sending an email, send energy to your Reiki Chakra. I always find it best to spend some time re-reading an email, even speaking it out loud quietly to myself.

When it comes to people and relationships, no matter how you say no, it may be that you have to end the relationship of someone you know or have known but who is no longer part of your life, but they have left a legacy that still brings them into your life.

It is best to be quiet and have a piece of paper and pencil Infront of you. Write their name at the top of the paper. If your writing is not that clear, write the name slowly and clearly.

Underneath write – "I release this person and attached emotions and all forms of connection from my life with love and peace." I find that drawing the Reiki Power symbol Cho Ku Rei in the centre of the page with smaller versions in each corner help to seal the words and the wishes. You can burn the paper, shred it and put it in the Recycling.

When you choose to do this it maybe that you do not have pencil and paper conveniently available. I put my hands together in Gassho and say the person's name and the words three times. I draw the Reiki Power Symbol, Cho Ku Rei, three times as I say the person's name and draw the symbol in the air with my finger.

In all of this, setting boundaries is not a selfish act, it an act of self-assurance and love for yourself. As you respect others it is only writing and fitting that you receive respect from others. Oh, and by the way, the same goes for family members. When we are young, it is OK to let parents set some of our boundaries, but as we mature and become adults, it is time for us to set our own.

25. Karma and Reiki

arma and Reiki. Karma is all about what goes around comes around, or you reap what you sow. Both imply that if you do good thigs, good things will come to you.

Karma operates through the law of cause and effect, action and reaction, it governs all life and binds the atman the Self, to the wheel of birth and death.

The process of action and reaction on all levels — physical, mental and spiritual - is karma. God does not give us karma. We create our own. Karma is not fate; humans are believed to act with free will creating their own destinies according to the Vedas, a large body of religious texts originating in ancient India.

If an individual sows' goodness, he or she will reap goodness; if one sows evil, he or she will reap evil. Karma refers to the totality of mankind's actions and their associated reactions in current and previous lives, all of which determine the future. However, many karmas do not have an immediate effect; some accumulate and return unexpectedly in an individual's later lives. The conquest of karma is believed to lie in intelligent action and dispassionate reaction.

As we move through many different lives, we also collect baggage, energies we carry form life to life. Some of these may be called Karmic debris, things that have an effect in this life that result from something in previous lives. Karmic diseases are often referred to as spiritual diseases for they are manifested only on a non-material-spiritual (simply Energy) level and materialistic methods cannot identify, describe or eliminate them.

Cleansing our Karma with Reiki is a gentle form of Reiki, and it is deeply personal to you.

The Reiki symbols to be used during the session where you heal the Karmic Fragments. Will depend on what you are attuned to.

Chu Ku Rei, the power symbol will be used to add extra energy and force to the other symbols you will use. If you are attuned at level II, Hunshazishuneen, the distance symbol will be used to help cross any spiritual distances the healing session may need to cross. Sei He Ki is used for mental energy and healing and accessing the subconscious and calming the mind and emotions.

To perform the healing session, you need to be clear in your mind what is not working. Trauma and injury in a past life, can lead to illnesses and inability to perform in the present life. For example, a limp may be medically explained as a problem with development of muscles, tendons, and joints. But the real course can be further back in a past life. The healing session may not be able to repair the damage, but it can make it easier. A negative relationship from the past can lead to imperfect relationships in this life, or, a type of relationship that is a "payback" for a previous life with an unsatisfactory relationship.
Focus on the issue and apply Chu Ku Rei to your thoughts and intention to repair the karmic debt which is making life difficult in this life. Draw it in the air in front of you.

Apply Hunshazishuneen to your intentions allows the energy to traverse across time between now and then the cause happened. Draw it in the air in front of you.

Use Sei He Ki to quieten and stabilize your thoughts and help keep your intentions focused. If you feel emptions rising up in you as a result of your efforts repeat Sei He Ki to help stabilize and quieten your mind and feelings. If you start to cry or have an outburst during the session, allow it to happen and let it pass. Do not try and stifle it. Draw it in the air in front of you.

At the end of the session, again, focus on the end of the issue and apply Chu Ku Rei to your thoughts and intention to complete repair of the karmic debt which is making life difficult in this life. Draw it in the air in front of you.

Sit quietly and think about what has happened. Think of your intentions and the future you want for yourself without the Karmic Debit.

26. Let Go

Every year in the spring, we clean our homes and when it comes to clothes and other possessions, we rarely use we make a decision whether to let go of them or keep them for another year. Well, that is the way it used to be, I am not sure whether in today's packed life, we have time to carry out the cleaning and let go of clothes and other possessions as they used to do say 60 years ago. Rather we go through clothes and possessions on an adhoc basis, when we have time or something sparks our need to do so, such as moving to a new home.

Even if the If we don't let go of our possessions, one thing is for sure, we rarely go through our personal and emotional attachments. By not doing so we won't solve our emotional problems and never be free of relationships that should have ended a longtime ago.

Old relationships, ones that are no longer part of our lives will always bring back some form of anxiety. A relationship that failed may cause feelings of depression, anger – at the other person as well as ourselves. The relationship will never fully disengage form us if we keep on bringing these emotions and feelings back to the surface by not letting go the original feeling.

Reiki energy will help you relax and in that comfortable state you will give yourself permission to start releasing those negative thoughts and emotions and the original seed that causes them.

Each morning and each evening I open myself to my angels and guides. They are there to help us, all they need is our permission to help. As all humans have free will, they cannot engage with us until we are open and receiving. Invoke Reiki energy through them to help you clear away these negative thoughts and the emotions they generate.

In the evening I have time to add to the list of negative thoughts and emotions any that have arisen during the day. That is when I focus on the thoughts and emotions that need to be released. I especially take time to consider what these things have generated inside of me.

Through the angels and guides, channel Reiki Energy to the thoughts and feelings that need releasing. I use my intention to Let Go of these feelings and to return to a balanced state. Slowly, the feelings and their causes will fade away and become a distant memory.

As with all things, letting go may be difficult and many things will be entwined with the original thoughts and deeds. It may take more than one session to get rid of all aspects of the feeling. Let it take that long, but always allow Reiki the time to heal you and bring new energy to the healing you are feeling.

At the end of the day, invite your angels and guides to join you in your dreams and to leave things behind that you can remember when you wake up. When you wake up check with yourself if there are any messages. If there are, do they apply to your feelings and emotions that you released yesterday or do they show you something new, something you can action or will be coming to you as a result of letting go!

27. Worries, Uncertainties, Worries and Uncertainty

Fears, Doubts, Worries and Uncertainty we all have them. They are the things that either separately or in combination stop us from moving forward and grasping the things we want and need. We are fearful when we move to a new job, will we excel as we did in the previous one. We worry about things we cannot control, and we are uncertain about what we should do next.

Dreams and aspirations are our expectations and hopes for a better future but sometimes we doubt we are capable of living those dreams. If we dream of a new car, will we be able to drive and park it as well as the old one we are driving?

A sunny condo overlooking a lake, or a cottage in the country, set amongst the trees and by a lake where we can boat, are we deserving of such beauty homes?

Buying a property comes with a lot of changes but also a lot of legal and other contractual things we have to complete before we can move in and make them our home, our beautiful relaxing home. Dwelling too long on all the things we have to do tends to take the shine off our vision for a bright and happy home.

Worrying about creating and manifesting the things we want and hope become stressful and wastes and hurts our soul.

Get in touch with the soul inside of you. Become yourself, put away the fears, doubts, worries, and uncertainties. Things you wish for are not out of reach when you get in touch with your true self.

Fears can be overcome by feelings of positivity. If you want that condo by a lake, think of yourself there and what life would be like, for you, for your pets, for others in your life. Would they visit you more often because you have a nice balcony to sit out on? Would the summer breezes be sweeter with the smell of the water? Thinking of these and any other enjoyable attributes of being in the condo become positive affirmations at put the fears away.

Doubts about being able to park the new car can disappear when you think of all the other people who drive the vehicle and park it easily, so why are you doubting your ability? Banish the doubts. Perhaps have a test drive in your chosen vehicle and try parking it?

Worries over the legal and contract issues for buying the property you wish are things many other people engage in. If you are a new buyer, so are many others, they get through the process. You are as capable as they are. They have worries too but maybe they do not show it. So, don't dwell on your worries, put them away and concentrate on doing everything you are required to easily and confidently.

Uncertainty. Well, nothing is certain. But uncertainty should not stop you from attempting something. Follow the guidance provided to everyone, gain confidence by doing. Until you have that experience of doing you will always have a little uncertainty.

Understanding this, sit quietly for a moment with your favorite incense burning and watch the smoke rise and how even small energies in the air of your room make the smoke stir and change direction. Think of the smoke carrying your wishes and desires to the universe.

If you are attuned to Reiki, sit with your hands in Gassho, still your busy mind and open yourself to Reiki energy and ask it to help you manifest your desires. If you are not attuned, ask the universe to help you manifest your desires. Attuned or not, be open and undemanding, be still and peaceful.

Picture *How* manifestation of your desire would bring peace and blessings to you first, and then to others? Picture all of this in your third eye. This is powerful because when our desires bring blessings, the Universe provides us immense support.

Let how you feel when the thing you are focused on makes you feel. Even though you are still "seeing" what it is you want to manifest I your Third Eye, it is important to know how you feel. I know that when [not if] my condo manifests I will spend time being amazed at the flow of the clouds across the sky and in stormy weather, how the energy in the storm will stir the water. Although there is so much energy in the weather, I know I will sense joy and peace.

Allow the emotions to recede and if you are attuned to Reiki, draw the symbols in the air in front of you, with your hands. Then clap your hands three times and let the session end naturally.

If your incense is still burning watch how it is burning down and sit still until the incense is burned out and gone.

This is a good practice to carry out before going to bed and getting a good night's sleep. Your mind is peaceful, and you have clarity about what it is you want to manifest and how it will make you feel. Your mind and your dreams, literally now, your dreams will be part of the process of manifesting because you have added clarity to manifestation.

28. Loving

Reiki is a powerful, intelligent energy, it is the universal energy of the universe. Once it has been invited into your life, it does many things for you. The one we are talking about here is helping you become aware of love. It opens your heart to be receptive to the loving things in life. Not just the people, but pets, and animals in general. It allows you to become sensitive to plants, trees and all other living things,

You start to relate to things in a loving and non-judgmental, and unconditional way. You begin to trust what you love and who loves you. We all have a soul and Reiki will help you connect with it in a way you have not been able to before. You become more energetically involved in life in a way you have not experienced before. That energy turns a previously reactive person into one that participates.

Our open connection to our soul, Reiki, the Universal energy is often referred to as "spiritual" and I for one was not aware of it. To me spiritual meant organized religion, and growing up in England that mean a Protestant faith, The Church of England. The church my family was associated with was built in the 1880's and that meant it was Gothic inside and out. The interior was dark and mysterious. The Alter and the Choir though were lit up like performers on a stage.

Today, spirituality is a broader term includes Reiki and alternative beliefs. It is widely available to any who are open to receive and understand it. To be connected to Reiki is not restricted to some spiritually advanced person, there is no hierarchy of Reiki clergy who administer rituals that only some can participate in.

Yes, there are somethings that go along with Reiki. Meditation or the ability to sit quietly and separate your mind an essence from the daily grind is one of them. But we should be doing that anyway, to help us detach and become rested and peaceful. Always living in high gear is not good for us.

Reiki does not require deep spiritual connection or practice. There are no mantras to be learned and practised, no prayers to be said every day. But there is connection and attachment. Faith and belief in Reiki, belief in ourselves and an openness that is required and cannot be given up. Perhaps that can be summed up by saying, we are already spiritual enough for Reiki, we are as perfect as we need to be and the energy knows that but it asks that we do not stop to see the beauty and help we bring to the world through our connection and how we use it – to heal.

The ego, the busy mind will always try to be front and center, to push Reiki and its living energy to one side so that in can monopolize our attention. It magnifies the challenges we face every day, every week, every month, every year. It will seek to disconnect us from Reiki. Reiki will be patient; it will wait for us to come back to it and once again become the center of our life by helping us to put our busy mind in its place. There is only one love and one fear, as we move though our lives, we move between these two forms of existence so when fear and worry exist in us, we become disengaged from love. This love, Reiki, is our natural state of being because it helps us be totally present in each moment of our lives.

Reiki energy combines our authentic nature with trust and allows us to experience our true self. When we are in this state, we can engage in intimacy with more authenticity and joy, we are more honest in our relationships and compassionate.

Be willing to open your heart and allow vulnerability to be your partner in exploring the Reiki and your inner soul, your inner world and without judgement or the need to hide or change or to accommodate others.

Working with Reiki brings an understanding of your natural ability for healing. This has to begin with you. We mirror and reflect who we are in others; our pain can be seen in every person you meet. When we heal ourselves, we are able to guide the healing process for others. There is an assimilation that takes place as you witness the flow of energy available to all, not to a chosen few or a spiritual elite.

Reiki is yours, everyone's, it is waiting…

29. Listen to your intuition, not your ego.

ur soul comes with an ego, it helps us look after ourselves in the material world. There are many definitions of ego; here I will try to explain it from personal experience, rather than drawing from the literature or academic ideas.

The role of the ego is twofold – it protects us, and helps us tell ourselves apart from other people.

Our soul is expansive, energetic and creative; it defies logic, shifts and changes happen in bursts and growth occurs quickly.

In contrast, our ego is logical, slow to change, evidence based and looks for proof and validation before accepting anything to be true.

Our ego reflects the opinion we hold of ourselves, but that opinion changes slowly over time as the ego shifts to accommodate what we believe. Think of our opinion of ourselves as including:

- Self-esteem is how much we like ourselves.
- Self-worth is how much we value ourselves.
- Self-confidence is a belief in ourselves and our abilities.

Society is based around the ego – it keeps us on our toes and functioning in the world that we live in. We are part of the crowd and generally don't stand out by doing anything special, or that can be criticized…

To not stand out from the crowd we need to repress something in ourselves. We need to hold back our gifts, our talents, our truth. When this happens, we become disconnected with our true essence, with our "selves" and that's where a lot of the pain in life comes from. As we get lost in the mix, we forget who we are, or that we have a right to be happy. We struggle to reconcile what the ego tells us and what intuition, our real selves wants to do or say.

The ego makes things more important to us when they really are not. We become submissive, we're told what to do, and who to be, and to do it without questioning it. The system of our society is based around the ego, we are living the ego, and in that, everyone is following everyone else.

STOP IT!!!! Listen to your heart, listen to your energy body, to your soul. Listen to what is you want to do, go where your heart and your intuition lead.

The ego has a role to play in our lives, we need it but we need to have control over it rather than be under its control.

Learn to act on your intuition and bring it to the front of your attention. Don't hold back on your gifts, talents, or your truth. Open up and express them, listen to that inner voice that tells you to try something new.

30. Mindset

The COVID-19 pandemic is affecting the planet, there are few who have not heard of it by now and over 20 million cases and nearly 750,000 deaths according to the most recent tally - 2020/08/10. It is also affecting our mindset.

Countries are in lockdown, or, just coming out of it and millions have lost their jobs. Simply traveling by public transit, which we were always encouraged to do to cut down on driving and emissions from cars is now fraught with rules – masks are mandatory, and we increase the risk of contracting the disease from handrails and our fellow commuters.

I know it is informational and interesting, and as part of the greater public, we do need to know the current state infections in our communities, but it is also depressing and worrying when day after day, things show little change and perhaps change in the wrong direction.

There is a continued stress on our minds, our souls and spirits when we see these reports over and over again. It is our mind, the greatest and most powerful tool we have to help us through the trials of this special year 2020.

As they say, "Healthy Mind, Healthy body." When our mind is at ease and is receiving healthy, stimulating and interesting information and stimulation our bodies are healthy. No doubt part of healthy stimulation is social interaction, but we need to think of social interaction in new terms. A friend of mine, who has been retired for a long time, and who infrequently called, and rarely met, has discovered FaceTime on her Mac and iPhone and now we chat more than ever before – almost weekly. Social interaction does not mean in person, and we need to recognize that.

Recognizing that, our interaction can help with all manner of things; we can talk and see someone to discuss things that have happened if stressful, we can relieve stress with another. If happy and positive, we can share our joy and happiness. Both types of news when shared help us to be at ease and relaxed. Life is good!

One thing my friend and I do at the end of a FaceTime chat is to check with each other that we are "good" that there is nothing else we are bottling up inside of us that can affect our outlook on life and ourselves.

Here are a few thoughts about how we can look at our lives, what is happening and our feelings toward it.

Don't resist, accept what is happening to us. If we can't change it, why are you worrying? If that sounds too casual for a situation where you are worried about paying the rent or buying groceries, look at this way. Worrying, and allowing yourself to become stressed out elevates your worry to a new level so that when your busy mind returns to the topic, it starts with from a new intensity that leaves you even more depleted.

When I first realized my connection to Reiki, my angels, archangels and guides, the best and most beneficial aspect I learned was to give up my worries to them and ask for their help in becoming more at peace with my situation. I also learned to listen to them when they had something to say to me. Although I am more practiced in that dialogue now, I will often sit in a quiet place, close my eyes and give up all the thoughts I worry about. I also ask for their help and guidance in matters which can be summed up as "Healthy, Wealth, and Happiness."

Breathing is essential to our lives. We need to take in air and expel the used air. When we stop breathing, stop the process of filtering Oxygen from what we breathe in and expelling carbon dioxide, that is the first indicator that we have passed over to a new life. That is, we are dead.

Breathing is rhythmical. When we lie in bed before we go to sleep, we can sense it. The pace of breathing becomes quicker if we are exercising. We can use that rhythm like a metronome, just like a mechanical device we can concentrate on it and reconnect with our physical being, and if outdoors, where it is peaceful, such as in a park, we can listen to the birds and animals going about their lives. All are positive experiences.

When I first realized my connection to Reiki, my angels, archangels and guides, the best and most beneficial aspect I learned was to give up my worries to them and ask for their help in becoming more at peace with my situation. The next thing I realized was to thank them for the help and support they were giving me. Giving gratitude for help form the universe is a wonderful, enriching thing for your soul.

When I leaned that I also started saying to thank you to me. I did this after I woke up in the morning and just before I went to bed. There is a soul in me that is here to learn lessons from my physical existence. Mother Earth, Gaia, brings me a lot of good things and some that are not but I learn from all of them. I am grateful and I now show gratitude for all things, but especially for who I am.

I find a quiet space and for a moment, hand over heart, I thank "Me" for who I am and what I have learned. When I say what I have learned, I do not have a big list, maybe a few notable events of the day, or night, if I had some interesting dreams. I believe in keeping this simple, but honest, own your life and what I say, or, do not say, what I do, or, do not do they are all part of the soul's learning in this life.

When I first realized my connection to Reiki, my angels, archangels and guides, the best and most beneficial aspect I learned was that becoming attuned to Reiki, I can help others by providing Reiki energy to them. In today's world, this is remote Reiki, but Reiki is intelligent energy, it is Universal energy it knows how and where to go to be supportive of the recipient. In the same way, self-Reiki, can be equally beneficial. Trust Reiki.
Perform Reiki as you would for a recipient but instead, you are the focus. Do you have a backache, ask for help in healing what is causing the problem? Did you fall and break your arm, ask for help in healing the bones? The self-Reiki session is performed in exactly the same way as you would do for an in-person session; open it, conduct the session and close it just as you would normally.

At the end of it, thank you, for taking care of you. And, while you are at it, tell yourself something… Tell you that you love who you are.

31. New Year's Resolutions.

New Year's resolutions are traditionally made at the start of the year. After all, this what they are called. That is when we set out our expectations and desires for the coming year. When we create these resolutions, they should be more than just wishes or desires.

We need to add intention to each of the wishes, we need to add "how" to achieving our wishes. We cannot swim if we have not first overcome any feelings of fear about getting in the water, having our face covered with the liquid, or learned the mechanics of moving our arms and legs to propel us in the water.

It is OK if there are some resolutions that are just wishes with no how. Not knowing how something will be attained does not make it any less of a of a resolution.

Once we have set our resolutions, we need to consider them. Are the goals expressions of loving, enrichment for ourselves and others we acre about? Call on you angels to ask if the resolutions are in tune with your life purpose? Be open to message from your angels that change the goals, change the intentions or show you a new way to achieve your resolution.

If you are attuned to Reiki, use the energy from Reiki to guide you through the process and infuse energy into the resolution.

Having trouble getting started or completing a resolution? Sit quietly and focus on your resolution and Reiki energy. Allow Reiki to give you energy and strengthen your resolve to attain your goals. If you are feeling negative, allow it to change the negative feelings to positive ones.

If the negative feelings persist, use Reiki to look at and uncover any underlying issue that has not been dealt with. I have immensely enjoyed my time as a Scuba diver and as an Instructor passed that joy on to others. But for a long while I allowed others from preventing me form taking courses and get started as a diver. It was when I stopped allowing other people's fear to control my desires that I took my first courses and was hooked on the diving.

Now! Making resolutions about what we want to do in life should not be confined to the beginning of the year and one set of resolutions. Make them continuously through the year, and if a resolution has not completed, simply let it carry on. Don't discard it, use Reiki energy to restart the resolution if necessary and include it with all the new goals you have set for yourself.

If you are not attuned to Reiki yet, book a Reiki session to help you.

Then, start studying Reiki and become attuned as a new resolution. Let Reiki help you along your life path purpose and your connection with your angels and guides.

32. New Experiences and Reiki Energy

As a Reiki professional – a Registered Reiki Teacher and Practitioner, I like to find new ways to energize myself.

Energy can come in many ways, courses, workshops and group meetings where I can sense the energy vibrations of others. But there are other ways to energize myself.

By a lake near me I have "my spot" somewhere I call mine but is really a public location with a comfortable public bench. It is on one of the public pathways but few if any people seem to get to. I can sit there, watch the sun come up, watch the water, and all the birds flying in the air. I feel the breeze, I can sense the nature angels as they encourage the plants, trees and flowers to grow. Best of all, I can commune with my personal angels and guides.

The whole ecosystem in the park is based on natural growth with minimal human intervention. I love it and it is a place I have taken many photographs and spent a lot of time looking at the insects that inhabit the place.

There is also a highbacked chair in my home office that never strays from in front of my computer. It is where I write, where I edit my images and when I have sot a video about Reiki or Shamanism, or recorded a Podcast I can work on them so I can share them with the world.

Just sometimes, there are people walking in the park that I start a conversation with. They are energized and open. They are interested and invigorated by the same things as me but their connection may be a little less spiritual.

The park is a good place to perform a self-Reiki session. Nature, life, and all kinds of giving are all around you in nature, a flow is giving, it is giving nectar, scent, pollen and beauty. Drink up that energy. For those of us on the Reiki path, regular Reiki self-healing is certainly one of the easiest ways to use the time at "my spot." The energy around me is abundant and the connection with my guides, that more intense.

Such places, a bench by the water of a large lake, or at a computer, are special places. At the bench I receive and learn to understand the abundance around me and how it helps me. At the computer, I learn to share, to provide, to give. I learn to express ideas, thoughts and experiences in ways that others can comprehend.

Think of ways you can absorb the core energy of the universe that is Reiki and then share it with family and friends. If you are attuned, the added energy in your sessions will help you're your recipients and yourself as there will be more to give.

33. My Start with Reiki

ver the years I have had Reiki sessions form a number of practitioners. All sessions were incredibly beneficial to me, I always felt at peace with myself and my life for weeks and months after.

But it was the last practitioner who mentioned I had a skill, something useful to others that I was unaware of. It would be a new path for me. She moved on to follow her own path but left me with a very beneficial contact who would help me follow my new path.

I was attuned to Reiki Level 1 shortly after I meet my Registered Reiki Teacher and Practitioner. My studies with Reiki, the history, the vibrancy of Reiki energy, the clarity of thought and purpose it gave me and the desire to help others encouraged me to continue with added purpose and vigor. I am attuned to Master Teacher Level and I too am a Registered Reiki Teacher and Practitioner under the Canadian Reiki Association and A Usui Tibetan Reiki Master Teacher under the International Association of Reiki Professionals.

Attunement happens as part of your studies at each Attunement level. It is performed by a Reiki Master. It takes minutes to complete and is different for every person. You may feel or become aware of Reiki energy or you may not. In my case, my connection with the new Reiki Symbols and energy that I received in the Attunement happened after the event, when I was at peace in my own space. There was a sense of a new width to my connection to Reiki and awareness that when needed, that width would be taken up by Reiki.

Following attunement, it is sometimes the case that the new energy we are receiving unblocks and releases stuck energy from the body. Energetically, it also removes energy that no longer meets our purpose. The remains of a relationship that did not work out is removed at this time. Depending on how receptive you are, how much stuck energy there is, and how much energy baggage you are carrying around with you, this clearing can take some time.

I was fortunate, the time and the effects of the energy clearing were minimal. As the days passed, my link to this powerful energy became stronger and gave me a sense of purpose and I came to understand the direction I was to follow, what my life path purpose is.

Connecting to Reiki changes everything. Colors are deeper and richer, especially when I am out in nature, walking in the park. When I am in the park and stop on a bench, it is because I am feeling my connection to nature and everything round me is deeper. There is a feeling that all around me is energy, it is growing and diverse, and will always be there. I understand that all creatures are sentient beings, all are energetic and each has a spirit and is connected to the universal energy as we are becoming aware of. We are part of nature, not an observer or by stander of nature.

Intuition and intention expand. I have a broader relationship with the world and who I interact with every day. Increasingly, there is a sense of being awakened to this wonderful physical world and to the spiritual, energetic world.

Over time, this connection with the natural world matures and we understand that all creatures are sentient beings and we connect with them on a much deeper level. We become part of nature, as opposed to being simply an observer of nature. We learn to live in harmony with all beings. We learn the way of love and light.

34. Mother Earth of Gaia

So many things are affecting the planet we live on. Mother Earth, or Gaia [I will use Gaia from now on] is heavily affected by all that Mankind is doing. Each one of us shares responsibility for our actions that affect her. Even something as simple as throwing bottle or can into the bushes rather than holding on to and disposing of it properly.

As an example, that bottle or can throwing into some bushes soils and dirties the plants growing there, provides somewhere for disease and insects to grow and is not recycled as it should be resulting in more minerals taken from Mother Earth which is unnecessary.

Gaia nurtures, and grounds us. She provides the water we drink and a place to sleep. She provides land for us to grow our crops and our animals. Day after day, month after month, year after year she does this and forgives the mistakes we make and provides for us unconditionally by granting us a new season to grow what we need.

When we are attuned to Reiki, we can perform a simple self-Reiki session, it only takes 10 minutes a day, either at the start or end of the day. It calms our worried minds and thoughts.

When we are sitting quietly and asking Archangel Michael to stand guard over the session, to protect the session from any dark or lower energies, any energies that should not be there. That is the time to ask Gaia to participate in the session.

As you settle down to the self-Reiki meditation draw the Reiki Symbols over our chest and ask Gaia to lend energy and potency to the session for ourselves. Be open to Gaia communicating with you, sometimes in words, other times in colors and images. On some occasions, Gaia will be provided feelings such as heat and warmth to help with the session.

Because this is a self-Reiki session, any information, feelings or information you have received from Gaia is for you alone.

As always, at the end of the session, thank your Reiki Guides and angels and archangels, and all who support us and the session that has just ended. Thank Gaia for joining. Thank Archangel Michael for guarding the session.

Reiki is a spiritual journey; it is not a discipline. Be accepting of the unexpected gifts and benefits that Reiki brings you. If you decide you will ask Gaia to help you in your next self-Reiki session, accept what gifts she gives you and how she helps you. As you ask for her help more often you will become comfortable with her and the way she communicates. Eventually, the time will come for you to ask her to help when conducting sessions for others.

35. More Energy is Coming

More Energy is coming. Since being attuned to Reiki One, inside we have been changing. Each day, Reiki has been helping us, clarifying our intuition, guidance, our feeling and our thoughts. We have more control over our raging ego driven mind now, and if you are attuned to Reiki Two or Reiki Three, we think of ourselves and say we are more aware, healed, present, in contact with ourselves. As we learn to recognize the changes within ourselves over time, the effects of Reiki become more potent and clearer.

Some might say the changes on the inside are not reflected on the outside, the face, hands and feet we show to the world all look the same. If we have wrinkles or scars, accept them for what they are, they are part of our existence. The events that gave us those scars and wrinkles brought us to the point where we decided to change. We changed by becoming attuned. What is important is the smile of recognition of that change in us that Reiki brought to us now brings different people, and different habits into our lives.

When you get up each morning, take a moment to tell yourself, hand over your heart, that "you love and appreciate who you are." Do the same before you go to bed, perhaps calling out something that happened during the day. Was what happened "good" or was how you reacted to something bad, "good". Take that moment to consider how good you were and thank yourself.

Once you are attuned, even to Reiki 1 you have started a journey. Your life's journey has a soul partner, Reiki. It will always be inside of your, helping and encouraging. It will be there to guide and help you learn. Let it!

When you let Reiki help and encourage you it becomes more in tune with what you as a physical being need, it adjusts to us. So, shrug off your old thoughts and habits. They no longer serve you, and you no longer need them. Make yourself open to receive the new. When you put your hand over your heart and tell yourself you love yourself, feel the changes in your "self" take place; self-value, self-worthiness, self-esteem, and self-confidence are all enhanced, new and vibrant. Let no one tell you are not more confident, that your self-esteem is not more potent and energized.

You have started a journey and you have done well, and reached a cross roads, continue on the path of light and love and let Reiki guide you and journey with you.

36. Reiki Positivity Release stress

Reiki Attunement, at any level increase our sensitivity and connection an energy of a higher vibration. Reiki energy is pure, healing, and increase our sensitivity to all living things around us.

The Covid-19 pandemic has increased our collective worry and anguish about our lives, politics, the environment, and our families. Without a vaccine, or other medical healing available, the risk of contracting the virus is very serious.

Out of all of this, we need to see how we can forge new beginnings, and that in itself is stressful.

To create new beginnings requires change, in who we are and what we are doing. We must change how we recognize and work with others, who themselves, are in the process of changing. Change never creates comfort, there is always a certain level of discomfort, because discomfort is what makes us move forward.

Feelings of discomfort and anxiety, within yourself, or the outside world can be reduced if you have a Reiki practitioner who is able to provide Reiki distance healing, and self-healing for accidents and things that happen in your life. The benefits of distance healing will help reduce anxiety and stress.

Positivity in the face of anxiety and stress can help reduce your inner unease. Send out these thoughts and feelings to those around you, even pets. They pick up on the stress and worry of us humans. They need some comfort and feelings of positivity. Ask your angels and guides for help in relieving you of what worries you.

Talk to and with your Reiki practitioner to understand how you can send your feeling of happiness and balance out to the greater world.

Learn to be more Mindful and in the moment. Reduce the ability of your busy mind to take over and churn about things you cannot change.

Learn to meditate, even if only for a few minutes, that is long enough for you to start feeling the benefit of detaching and being more in the moment. Combine your meditation with Mindfulness to get the most benefit.

Then, practice both so that your meditation time is longer and more mindful.

Check out our eBook and paperback book on Mindfulness

Repeat your attention to Reiki and its Five Principals daily and meditate on them to bring their values into focus.
Go out into nature each day of you can. Even if you cannot spend a lot of time in nature, recognize the animals and the growing and living things around you when you are able to.
I prefer to be out by water, trees and places where animals and insects can live without the hand of man being noticeable. Nature is an energy source and recharges and nourishes your soul.

Use Reiki self-healing to create moments of calm and peace of mind.

Create a sanctuary – This is a place where you can disconnect from social media, the news, and the barrage of the busy world. It is a place where you can be at one with yourself. If you are able to meditate do so, if you are able to be mindful and, in the moment, use the space and the time to practice more deeply.

When someone does something nice for you, even if you don't know them. Say thank you. Gratitude is often returned, if not immediately, it can be found the next time you encounter that person.

Don't forget that you make a difference in other people's lives. Don't think you do not. Many small changes by you help make larger changes for all around you. Be an inspiration by focusing on the positives.

Repeat the Reiki Principles – channel your energy into understanding each of them and how they affect your everyday life. Stay focused on them with heart felt appreciation and give yourself permission to be as happy as you can be.

37. Reiki and Home Life

Reiki and our Home Life, when we were born, we were born into a family, at least for most of us that is. But even if we were not born into a flesh and blood family, there will be caregivers around us and a place we can call sanctuary.

The family is a container, a place containing people, warmth, security and a space where we can be away from others. It is a place we exist in for many years as we grow and develop. It is the first place where we learn to interact with others and understand their responses to us.

It is a place of love and energy, where we show our successes and ask for help with our failures. It is also a pace where we learn to detoxify ourselves of the stress and strains, we endure during each day of our lives. It is how we find purpose in the day and strength for the next day.

Reiki can be intensely helpful in the stages of life we go through as we grow. Reiki is an intelligent healing energy form the universe; it is all around us, and it is available to all of us.

If you are attuned to Reiki, you can help your family with Reiki energy. When I say family, I mean all of the family, not just the one who is in need of spiritual energy. Of course, if there is someone in need, yes, give them a Reiki session and energy. But all in the family are affected, give energy to them as well.

Before giving energy, always detoxify or spiritually cleanse who will receive Reiki. If you are not attuned to Reiki, a remote healing session can be organized for the family and the individual who most needs it. At Intothelight.xyz, we offer those sessions. The connection is remote, and without any contact.

Reiki, in person or remote can he used to help those who have a disease, or condition that affects all the family but manifests itself in one person. It can be used with conditions such as cancer, to help prepare the body before medical intervention, sustain the body during treatment and help heal it afterwards.

To extend Reiki energy to any group consider how you are attuned to Reiki. You need to be attuned to receive and use Cho Ku Rei, the power symbol and Hunshazishuneen pronounced "Hone sha say show nun" which is the distance symbol.

The session is intended to help each individual in the group and the group as a whole. Ask the guardian angels for each member of the group to be present and to assist with transmission of Reiki energy to the person they are spiritually connected to.

The session, as with all Reiki Sessions should be guarded by Archangel Michael. His power and wisdom should be invoked to protect the session form dark and lower energies, or any energies that might try and disrupt the session.
This symbol carries the meaning of "The Divine Power in me greets the Divine Power in you to promote enlightenment and peace." The direct translation is "The Buddha in me sees the Buddha in you". This symbol transmits Reiki across distance, space and time and is used primarily for distance healing.

NOTE: There is an integrity requirement for doing long distance Reiki as there is for doing hands-on Reiki and that is to get the person's permissions first. Distance Healing should never be done on someone without permissions, as they will feel it, and may not know what is happening to them and get upset. Hunshazishuneen is a bridge between two worlds, transcending time and space.

Hunshazishuneen can be used for other purposes other than during a Reiki session. Consider the following:

- It is the heavenly connection used to send absentee healing
- Always draw the symbol once and say the name three times
- It should always be used in combination with other symbols, especially Power Symbol which activates it
- It always comes first
- Use to send treatments to past, present, future or to other dimensions
- Use to tune into a person or situation
- It accesses the Akashic Records life records of each soul's many incarnations, karmic goals, debts, contracts and life purpose of each incarnation
- Past life patterns and karmic debts can be uncovered and released using the symbol during hands on treatment

After sending Reiki energy to each person in the group, switch focus to the group as a whole. As you do, ask each member's guardian angels to be present and help with the delivery and integration of Reiki energy with the individual.

At the end, concentrate on the group, all members together and send Reiki energy to the group, to let it help and heal the group interactions. Seal the session and send Reiki with Cho Ku Rei.

Always… always, thank Archangel Michael for protecting the session and close it.

38. Reiki Healing

Modern medicine differs from Reiki Healing. Modern medicine deals with problems, it provides solutions and methods and approaches intended to resolve the problem. If a bone is broken, it is reset and immobilized until new bone has grown and the break is sealed. When the immobilizing cast is removed some physio therapy is applied to regain muscle tone and flexibility. Batteries of tests can be performed to determine hormonal and other factors that appear in the blood as indicators of organ problems, or problems with the efficiency of the body.

The approach is very effective, in crisis situations, the desired resolution can be determined quickly and applied affectively as the procedures for both are well understood. With our fast paced, ego driven world, the quicker a problem can be determined and a solution applied the better. We can get back to our lives that much sooner. We tend to think in terms of procedures, pills, injections and surgery. This detaches us from the essential think we care about, our bodies, the container for our soul.

It is not that we have no responsibility for our health, but we have largely given over that accountability to someone else the doctor, or the pharmacist. We have placed the deciding vote about our health in the hands of others.

Reiki Healing has more to offer than reducing pain, supporting a person's soul during illness or boosting the healing process to make it more effective. This is all well and good, but it is also limiting Reiki Healing to a small role, it has much more capability. It has the capability to bring the mind and body together. The mind is a powerful tool to bring to the healing argument.

I had Reiki sessions several times before I started to study Reiki and eventually became attuned to Reiki and ultimately became a practitioner and teacher. In all cases, a Reiki session was like a deep meditative state. And, like a meditation session, I was not only rested but a lot of clearing had taken place which brought renewed sense of balance.

Balance from a Reiki session, is more than just applicable to anything that is wrong with our bodies in that moment. Removal of bonds and ties to the past, to shedding and removing bad habits and creating new links to healthier ways of living, mental attitudes that prefer the healthy over the unhealthy. Changing emotional connections and recognizing the connections that are not benefiting us and should be allowed to end. These healthier patterns are what we call Reiki Healing. As you recover form your broken arm or leg, these changes can help you heal quicker.

Perhaps the best outcome for a Reiki Healing session is the opening up of your mind and souls to the possibility of

We can release old emotional wounds more easily, becoming free of the energetic bonds to the past. Our minds can more easily rewire to healthier patterns of thought and behavior. Choosing a new path for our life, our relationships, our hopes and dreams and willingness to recognize what is good and bad in our emotional connections can set us on a new and healthier path. choose a new path.

There is one commitment you need to agree to, you need to have more responsibility for your own well-being and be motivated to take the steps forward as they become clear. This is your part of the bargain with Reiki Healing, it will help you if you help yourself.

Change is always uncomfortable, old habits die hard they say, so, some effort will be required by you as well. If you are overweight because of a bad diet and lack of exercise, Reiki Healing will help you recognize that and why you are that way but it will not stop you from buying a cheeseburger, and a big drink, instead of the salad, you have free will, it is up to you to make the choice and choose wisely from the menu.

Reiki is a Universal Life Force Energy. It is all around us, supporting our existence.

I kind of new this before I had my first Reiki Healing session but most people are unaware of it at all. The session brought the awareness of Reiki and the Life Force Energy front and center on my life. Don't just call on Reiki to for help when we are in pain, sick or have a problem, work with it, combine with it, all the time. Reiki is not outside of us; it is inside of us. We started this post talking about how we treat medicine and healing, we see that as a pill, a procedure, a drug, something that is outside of us and administered according to the instructions of someone outside on the outside.

Don't treat Reiki that way. Trust Reiki. Reiki is not a bandage, a pill, a drug, a procedure. It is not something you do on demand, when something is wrong. A Reiki Session is not just for when something is wrong with you. It is something you practice for yourself every day. Reiki offers clarity and growth.

39. Reiki Positivity Release stress

eiki Attunement, at any level increase our sensitivity and connection an energy of a higher vibration. Reiki energy is pure, healing, and increase our sensitivity to all living things around us.

The Covid-19 pandemic has increased our collective worry and anguish about our lives, politics, the environment, and our families. Without a vaccine, or other medical healing available, the risk of contracting the virus is very serious.

Out of all of this, we need to see how we can forge new beginnings, and that in itself is stressful.

To create new beginnings requires change, in who we are and what we are doing. We must change how we recognize and work with others, who themselves, are in the process of changing. Change never creates comfort, there is always a certain level of discomfort, because discomfort is what makes us move forward.

Feelings of discomfort and anxiety, within yourself, or the outside world can be reduced if you have a Reiki practitioner who is able to provide Reiki distance healing, and self-healing for accidents and things that happen in your life. The benefits of distance healing will help reduce anxiety and stress.

Positivity in the face of anxiety and stress can help reduce your inner unease. Send out these thoughts and feelings to those around you, even pets. They pick up on the stress and worry of us humans. They need some comfort and feelings of positivity. Ask your angels and guides for help in relieving you of what worries you.

Talk to and with your Reiki practitioner to understand how you can send your feeling of happiness and balance out to the greater world.

Learn to be more Mindful and in the moment. Reduce the ability of your busy mind to take over and churn about things you cannot change.

Learn to meditate, even if only for a few minutes, that is long enough for you to start feeling the benefit of detaching and being more in the moment. Combine your meditation with Mindfulness to get the most benefit.

Then, practice both so that your meditation time is longer and more mindful.

Check out our eBook and paperback book on Mindfulness

Repeat your attention to Reiki and its Five Principals daily and meditate on them to bring their values into focus.
Go out into nature each day of you can. Even if you cannot spend a lot of time in nature, recognize the animals and the growing and living things around you when you are able to.
I prefer to be out by water, trees and places where animals and insects can live without the hand of man being noticeable. Nature is an energy source and recharges and nourishes your soul.

Use Reiki self-healing to create moments of calm and peace of mind.

Create a sanctuary – This is a place where you can disconnect from social media, the news, and the barrage of the busy world. It is a place where you can be at one with yourself. If you are able to meditate do so, if you are able to be mindful and, in the moment, use the space and the time to practice more deeply.

When someone does something nice for you, even if you don't know them. Say thank you. Gratitude is often returned, if not immediately, it can be found the next time you encounter that person.

Don't forget that you make a difference in other people's lives. Don't think you do not. Many small changes by you help make larger changes for all around you. Be an inspiration by focusing on the positives.

Repeat the Reiki Principles – channel your energy into understanding each of them and how they affect your everyday life. Stay focused on them with heart felt appreciation and give yourself permission to be as happy as you can be.

40. Reiki for a Good Night's Sleep

Reiki for a Good Night's Sleep, yes sleep. We sleep every night, and sometimes we nap during the day, if we have the opportunity.

How much we sleep is not so important as how well, or the quality of the sleep we get. While some will sleep for eight hours, some for six or even less, and some for nine hours. When life is demanding, the time we sleep may vary. Someone used to sleep for six may suddenly start sleeping for eight hours.

It is all down to the quality of sleep we get. It is all down to what our body and our mind's need that drives the duration and the quality of sleep. This is why, people with busy hectic lives are often sleep deprived. They wake up after a night's sleep according to their alarm clock, not when their body is finished resting, because they have to, in order to get on with the chores and tasks of the day ahead.

Whenever I have a Reiki session, I feel so rested, and when I get home, it is a certainty I will get a restful sleep. But long before that session, years before that session I made a commitment to myself that I would take care of this container, this physical body my existence in this life depends on.

I would do good and beneficial things for it. Good exercise, good nutrition, good sleep, good relaxation. Do things that are interesting and stimulating and not allow toxic and stressful people into my life, and if they snuck in, evict them quickly. Above all, not to endure stressful and toxic places and work any longer than I need to.

I added a routine to my preparation for going to bed. To clear away all the burdens and events of the day so that none are carried over into my dreams. Sit quietly and ask Archangel Michael to be present and ask him to use his sword to cut any cords, attached to, my souls, my spirit, my physical self or my chakras. Then, I ask him to fill me with his pure white light and protect me with his energy.

I thank my guides for their help during the day and tell them I love them, but before that, I tell myself that I love me, I need to know that I am loved. We tend to go through life without recognizing what this body does for our spirit.

If I have any aches and pains, I treat them in a self-Reiki session. Aches and pains can be emotional, and they can be about the racing, ego driven mind. Calm and heal those types of aches and pains as well.

As I go into the bedroom, I see myself in a cocoon of healing peaceful energy watched over by my guides.

Because I may wake up in the evening, I ask one of my guides to help me get back to sleep quickly.

Last, I ask all my angels and guides to join me in my dreams and to leave any messages I need to know there for when I wake up.

41. Reiki Personal Clearing

Reiki Personal Clearing can help with Spiritual clearing, it is rather like a physical Detoxification program. Detox programs aim to clean your blood and eliminate harmful toxins from your body.

From a spiritual point of view, Reiki can do the same. We all need a spiritual cleanse from time to time.

A reiki Personal Clearing session can be performed by a qualified Reiki Practitioner if you are not attuned to Reiki energy. Reiki balances and cleanses your Chakras.

Whether or not you combine a physical detox program with a Reiki Personal Cleansing, is up to you.

A Reiki Personal Clearing is quiet time. It is time to sit quietly, with no distractions, if you are attuned to Chu Ku Rei, the Reiki Power Symbol, draw it it in front of you, and in the air in each direction of the space you are sitting in.

Close you eyes and slow down your busy mind, as your mind slows down it will clear until your mind is totally free of thoughts. Ask Reiki energy to help clear and then refuel your Chakras. Feel the energy flow from universe to each of your Chakras.

So not worry if the Chakras do not clear and refuel from the root to the crown. The Chakras are a circle of energy, as I say, "from the root to the crown, and from the crown to the root." Reiki energy will cleanse and refuel the Chakras in the order they need it but always making sure that all Chakras are full with potency.

During the process, if there are any thoughts that appear in your mind, do nothing with or about them. Let them pass without anything being done. If they are important, they will resurface at another time, this is your Reiki Personal Clearing session, that is all you are concerned with.

At the end of the session, draw Chu Ku Rei once again in front of you, and in the air in each direction of the space you are sitting in.

You can perform the Reiki Personal Clearing as often as you need, but each night as I lay in bed and before I go to sleep, I ask my Archangels to Clean and Balance my Chakras. This will help keep chakras balanced and clean, which means less work to do when you sit down for a deeper Clearing.

42. Reiki Chakra Energy

The Chakras are full of energy, Reiki Chakra Energy... exists in all 7 Chakras which form a conduit for energy to travel from the Root chakra to the Crown and from the Crown back to the Root.

Chakra	Color	Meaning	Crystals
Root	Red	Feelings of Safety and confidence	Red Jasper, Obsidian, Fire Agate, garnet, ruby, onyx, red jasper, obsidian, smokey quartz, jet stone, hematite
Sacral	Orange	Creative Expression	Carnelian, Orange Calcite, Golden Topaz, orange zincite, imperial topaz, mookaite, sunstone, moonstone
Solar Plexus	Yellow	Our personal Power	Citrine, Tiger's Eye, Yellow Labradorite, amber
Heart	Green	Love and Connection, a bridge between physical body and body, mind, emotions, and spirit	Jade, Moss Agate, Aventurine, Morganite, rose quartz, green and pink tourmaline, malachite, emerald
Throat	Blue	Verbal expression, thoughts as well as words	Blue Lace Agate, Angelite, Aquamarine, Lapis Lazuli, Sodalite, turquoise or blue lace agate, chrysocolla, Blue Kyanite, larimar, amazonite
Third Eye	Purple	Intuition	Lapis Lazuli, Sodalite, Azurite, Azurite, tanzanite, sodalite
Crown	Violet	Enlightenment, spiritual connection to our higher selves, others, and the divine	Amethyst, Labradorite, Selenite, charoite, clear quartz

Table 1. Chakras, meaning and associated crystals

Choosing crystals is a personal thing! When I choose crystals, I will work with I hold them in my right hand. As a conduit for Reiki energy, I receive with my right hand and give with my left. Some practitioners will be the opposite and some will receive and give energy with either hand. A crystal I can work with causes tingling in my right hand, where ever I place it.

But it is then up to me to take it home and clear it of any other energies it may have gathered from people who handled it in the shop or from other crystals it was next to.
I do this in conjunction with my guides. Archangel Michael is protecting the clearing season. The crystal is held between my hands which are in Gassho. I work with my Reiki guides until they tell me the crystal is clear. As an example, I purchased some small unpolished amethyst crystals. I held each against my third eye, and closed my eyes and cleared my mind.

In my third eye appeared TV Snow. Old TVs would display this "snow" when they had problems displaying pictures. Except in my mind all that would be white in the snow was violet, as I tried different crystals in this way, many would produce no effect, I bought only those that created this violet effect.

Crystals will help to focus Reiki energy into and clear the chakras of any blockages. You can use all the crystals at the same time, placing each over the chakra, or, only the crystals associated with the Chakras you are guided to.

If you are a Reiki Practitioner, and you are using the crystals with patients, clear the crystals after each session so there is no spiritual carry over from one patient to the next. If a patient brings their own crystals to use, ensure they understand what clearing the crystals is and check how they are preforming the ritual.

43. Reiki and Meditation

Meditation is a simple way to unclutter our minds and connect with ourselves. As we sit quietly, eyes closed, focused on breathing or some other sound that acts as a focus for our tireless minds, and the thoughts that busy mind brings to them. This time of peace and relaxation permeates our bodies through all the muscles, tendons, sinews, blood vessels and organs.

If you are attuned to reiki, mediation it is an excellent way to engage with your Reiki guides and Reiki energy. The closeness of your connection to your guides and the universal energy is important and should not be underestimated. When I am preforming a session, messages form my guides and Reiki energy are important to know and be able to understand the needs of the recipient.

The more we meditate and the more we connect with our guides and Reiki Energy, the fully and more powerful will be the connection and flow of essential energy.

To make the connection the usual meditation processes are followed. Note, that if you have a different process, follow that, we each are guided to follow a unique life path purpose, that path has subtle differences, requirements and needs. Our path provides equally subtly different benefits.

- Find a quiet setting, and either lay down or sit.

- Breathing, I personally do not take deep breaths or practice breathing in any special way. Rather, it is evenness and consistency of breathing that is important to me.

- I engage with my Reiki guides. It is always a pleasure to meet them and relax with them. The flow of energy that starts now is very relaxing yet strong and muscular.

- My guides understand my intention and what my needs are.

- At the end of the meditation, my guides will signify the end of the session so I thank them, and tell them I love them and slowly bring myself out of the meditation.

I journal every day and will record what took place, my experiences and any messages I was given. I am lucky in that my Reiki guides are very clear in their messages. If you have any doubts or confusion sit quietly and ask for clarification, focusing your mind on the question[s].

One thing, sometimes I find the messages I received are revisited in my dreams that night or a later night. Make sure you journal these thoughts and bring them together with any previous journal entries.

This type of session is for our own benefit if there are messages for a recipient we have worked with, or, will work with, record that as well and decide on how we will manage that information. But above all, use the messages given to you, for yourself. You are important in this session.

44. Reiki Spring Cleaning

Reiki Spring Cleaning! But it is summer, not spring. Reiki Spring cleaning can happen any time of the year, it is convenient to do it when spring starts because it is a time of year, we can easily calendarize. But Reiki Spring cleaning is not the same as the spring-cleaning ritual that clears out clutter and things we are no longer using, or, the physical cleaning of rooms, closets and carpets.

Reiki spring cleaning is a spiritual event. It can take place anytime and as often as we need our chakras cleared and aligned or the worries and concerns our busy, ego driven mind[s] keep driving us to care about.

COVID-19 and all the upset and changes it has brought for all of us this year has created a need for a Spiritual Spring Cleaning. There are several parts to a Reiki Spring Cleaning.

- Stop and meditate, or take a few moments to declutter your mind of your ego and all the worries and cares it demands we pay attention to. Let them go and shut off that tireless, worrisome, mind.

- Unless you reread it yesterday, take out your Reiki Student 1 manual. Start reading it, refresh your mind and your spirit.

- Read all of it, but pay attention to the Three Pillars of Reiki – Page 28

- Read and believe in the Dr Usui's Five Reiki Principles – Page 26

Think about your attunement, and look at your level1 certificate. Yes, it is a piece of paper, but like a door jam, it is holding up the moment when you became attuned and you became not just a receiver but a giver of Reiki. Those were exciting times, and you worked hard to study, to learn and understand so that the attunement could take place.

When you were attuned, you looked forward to level 2 and your greater Reiki journey and the start to a new existence, a more spiritual existence. An existence with something greater than you and which you could, through Reiki Sessions, share with others.

In the first bullet, I recommended shutting off and letting go of that busy, ego mind. If you have let that mind creep back into your daily life, now, in this spring cleaning is the time to practice and perfect releasing and shutting it down. It is a skill, a habit always worth perfecting.

Now that your mind is clear and your Reiki Spring Cleaning is underway. Set your intention for the next week, the next month to allow Reiki into your life more often. If you are attuned to Reiki 1, start motivating yourself to become attuned to Reiki 2, and look onward from level 2 to level 3. Reiki is a way of life and there are many things to learn, practice and share. Let the events of COVID-19 spur you on.

45. Goals and Manifesting dreams

oals and Manifesting dreams, for the future. Things we want to manifest that have a bigger meaning for us, whether it is a car, house, relationship, a big bank balance that infers security and peace of mind, or an academic qualification.

We also have a Things to Do list, for more mundane but never the less, important things. The grocery list that has things added to it so that I do not forget something I need and it stops me from buying things I do not need. Finally, the calendar items. Every Tuesday, I put out the green bin containing food scraps, on alternate Tuesdays, I put out either the Grey bin with garbage or the blue bin with recycling.

On our journey to manifesting something we want, such as an academic credential, there may be many parts or stages we have to progress through. Keeping track what we have to do to is important to reaching that bigger goal.

With so many things to do, we must organize how we keep track of the lists not just the things on them. With our energy going into so many things, we start to feel depleted and drained. Things we want to pay attention to suddenly do not have enough energy to devote to them. This can lead to frustration and confusion; a sense of chaos starts to overwhelm us and we resent where our energy has actually gone. If chaos, lack of energy and resentment about the scattering of our energy and our soul energy is strong enough we can become ill.

The healing energy of Reiki will help us quieten the chaos and help us to decide where and how we will devote our energy. It can bring balance and reinforce our intention to have a balanced and bountiful life that our soul enjoys by bringing to us experiences that are enriching and happy both in the short and long term.

Plan forward by simplifying the way you keep track of your plans, tasks and to do lists. I prefer to use automated tolls such as the calendar on my smart phone, when I create a task or add to a to do list, I enter how and when I want to be notified. That way I do not have to devote my energy to tracking and alerting myself to this or that or plan for the next step of something.

When tasks have been completed, let the day go, let the tasks go, the calendar will automatically delete them, I have done my best to fulfill my lists when I was alerted. To give me clarity and thoughtfulness, I carry with me crystals, White Zebra Jasper always, rose quartz, amethyst, citrine, and others as I feel guided. They will help me through the day and with any tasks, and to do list items I have to deal with.

As the tasks appear and are dealt with, I make sure to add any new responsibilities to my calendar as they appear. I do not want to deal with creating a new list when I get home at the end of the day. Remembering what you need to add to a to do list or my calendar, or creating a new to do list when it be done when it comes apparent is itself energy sapping. It creates anxiety and worry that you might forget it, get things in the wrong order, or create a to do list for the wrong thing.

At the end of the day sit quietly and thank yourself for the day and the attention you gave everything not just the things you had on your lists. Thank yourself for being you and tell yourself you love you! You have done and achieved all that you have with love, grace, and strength.

If you are attuned with Reiki, bring your hands together in Gassho and still your mind. Quiet that busy mind, quieten the ego. Concentrate on your energy and your Chakras. Concentrate on clearing and aligning your chakras so you have a powerful and clear flow of energy from your Root Chakra all the way to the Crown Chakra. Bring your intention to a having a good evening and a night's sleep that fill you with energy and allows you to wake tomorrow fully rested. Do not worry about tomorrow, you cannot change anything because it has not happened yet.

Amen.

46. Manifesting

e all need assistance in some way every day, now is the time to ask your angels and Archangels to help manifest it. Be clear about what you are asking for. They cannot provide help if they do not know what it is they are expected to help with or manifest.

For example, asking for help manifesting a new car is quite usual but too generic. A new car that is of a certain make, model or year, all are different. You might like a blue one, but accepting a vehicle that matches all the other requirements but is a different color is something you need to be flexible about.

Flexibility is important. If the universe and your angels' gift you something and you decline it because it "is not 100% right" you are telling the universe you are inflexible, you are looking at what is not rather than what is.

It is the old saying… "you get what you need, not, what you want."

One key thing to remember is to thank your angels sand guides when what you asked for has been manifested. Gratitude is a big part of the relationship between you, your ego, and your angels and guides.

47. A Vision Board

A vision board is a creative way to visualize the things you desire to manifest in your life.

Over the years I have created many vision boards, including ones that are text only. Some are image only and one that used software and payed back images and text as a "video."

The intention behind the vision board is that by creating it you solidify in your mind what you want to manifest. It is an act of reinforcement and communicating your desires to your angels and guides.

Vision boards can be for any purpose. The three big questions and desires most of us have are health, wealth, and happiness.

Wealth, a pot of gold! I envisaged wealth as a pot of gold, and where do you find post of gold usually? At the end of a rainbow. So, I found images of rainbows and pots of gold, I even printed out the claim form of a lottery corporation and put them all together on my vision board.

Health, for health I printed out pictures of myself when I was a lot less heavy and in better health. I watched YouTube videos of landscape photographers hiking long distances to take their images and wished to have good health and to be able to walk long distances like they did and photograph landscapes.

Happiness, means a female companion. I printed images of women that had the style or type that I felt I could live and like as a companion.

The images were all glossy, clean and I have a magnetic clip board so I could put them up in combinations that seemed to speak my needs and intentions at the time.

However, desires are not stand-alone needs, they interconnect with each other. Wealth would change my life styles, health and relationships, without recognizing them as being connected, I would not see how my life would change if each of them, or all of them were fulfilled.

Some will recommend that a vision board be very specific. A wedding wring with a particular stone setting might be desirable, but if your intended partner provides something different, accept it and do not be disappointed that the image has not turned into reality. It is the appearance of a ring that is important, not its style.

My most recent vision board has no immaculate images, it is all on one large sheet of paper, and rather than pictures of rainbows and pots of gold etc., it is hand drawn with stick figures and crude shapes.
As I drew each for my vision board, I realized there were smaller things that needed to be included. With a companion I take a much needed and better holiday than going on my own.

I drew a circle around each and showed how each connected to the other and those all connected to something else, rather like laces that close a shoe, the connections closed the small and big pictures into a whole.

I appear in each circle as a simple stick figure with the word 'Happy' next to me.

Things like health are indicated by simple words, 'fit, trim, and healthy.' The earlier board with images of me as I was in the past did not represent the now or the future. I am not interested I trying to relive or recreate an old me, I am interested in the new me that will come into existence.

The vision board in the end should not be perfect, it is the unexpected that brings amazing things to our lives. The risk of a perfect vision board is that what we receive may not match what we see on the wall. Remember to be accepting and not disappointed because life did not live up to a perfect image. Most definitely, do not ignore what is given to you.

48. Reiki Vision Board

What is a Reiki Vision Board? Well, traditionally it is some sort of board, a peg board, a cork board or a magnetic board onto which you can attach images and words that are motivational and express your desire for something.

That something may be material, physical, health related or spiritual. Usually it is something for yourself or your family.

The images and descriptions of what you want to manifest are guides not exact statements. The trick here is that if the universe manifests something for you that is on your vision board but is not exactly what is in the images and descriptions, do not be upset or unhappy at the difference. Be open to accepting what you are receiving, not what you wished for. If the vehicle you receive is grey, not white, accept it. If the engagement ring has three diamonds, not five but the diamonds are of better quality, accept the ring. And, take joy in it and thank the universe and your angels and guides for what has arrived.

Manifest this or something better now and for you [my] highest good. Energize the Law of Attraction!

What you have done with your vision board is make a statement and prepared your mind for your desires, but you have also created flexibility and openness for the difference that arrives. As an example, the last car that came to me was one I had never seen before, by a manufacturer I had not considered. I put the need and desire out to the universe along with the characteristic of the vehicle. Then I used a service provided by someone I knew who would hunt down a suitable vehicle. What arrived was and is perfect and has been for the past ten years.

To charge the vision board with Reiki, write out what you are feeling and why. If you are attuned to Reiki, add the power symbol to the beginning and end of your words. Add the symbol next to words or images that are important or significant to you.

Gently fold the paper in your hands and hold it in front of you while you ask the universe and your Reiki guides to add energy to what is on the piece of paper. Add that paper to the images and wishes on the vision board.

If you are not attuned to Reiki or only at Level 1, simply touch the vision board and quietly think of what it is you are manifesting.

One last thing. Write out your manifestation wishes, make them detailed and include small things, things that may have not made it on to the vision board on the wall. Roll up the paper and put an elastic band around them and put them in a drawer as a record of what you have just completed. Take the rolls of paper out from time to time and read them. When you have received something, check it off and say "Thank you!" then roll the paper up again and put it away.